Glamping as a Business

by

Samantha Lazzaris Newport

Published internationally by:

© 2015 Samantha Lazzaris Newport

Table Of Contents

Praise for Glamping as a Business

We've camped for many years with little or no facilities so staying with Sam in one of her Tipis was a step up to real comfort with beds and a little luxury! Glamping in the Algarve was the perfect way to relax and rejuvenate in the peaceful surroundings. Sam's book is easy to read yet full of useful information. It gives a peek behind the scenes at the hard work involved in creating your own piece of glamping paradise and a must read if you're thinking of making your glamping business dreams a reality.

Helen Taylor

Author of the crime thrillers – *Thai Die* and *Connecting Trains*

Director and owner of Tiny Treasures Gifts Ltd:
www.tinytreasuesgifts.co.uk

Preface

Over the years we have had many guests say that they are interested in setting up and running their own glampsite business and ask us how to do it. We are always happy to pass this information on and give some advice, as it is encouraging to know that there are other like-minded people out there wanting to enjoy a unique, sustainable business and lifestyle. People have said they could not find any books on setting up a glamping business, only on-line guides to glamping. I did some research and also found that there were no books that were specifically written on owning and running a glampsite business, so then I decided to write this book.

This is intended to be a practical guide for camping/glamping fans, owners and managers wishing to start from scratch through to maintaining a glampsite. If people have a piece of land they wish to transform and share with visitors, and make a useful income from it, then we can help you achieve this. Whether it is small scale, with one-unit accommodation, or a resort of 20 units, the challenges may be the same.

There is a lot of work involved with running a glampsite; it is a lot like setting up a campsite, along with the lovely touches found in a hotel or Bed and Breakfast (B&B).

Glamping was a new buzzword 10 years ago amongst the camping community (derived from 'glamorous camping'), but now it is very well known thanks to the media and the travel and tourism industry spreading the good word about glampsites throughout Britain and across the globe.

I hope you find this book useful in showing the steps you need to take to get your glampsite ready to open to trade and hopefully receive fruitful sales and revenue, and of course happy glampers! It may just put off some people in actually embarking on living the dream because of some of the nightmares that can accompany that dream. I wish to paint the real picture, not sugar coat it with bunting. Each chapter is peppered with examples and anecdotes of our experiences running our glampsite in the Algarve, Southern Portugal. Although I knew this book needed to be written to help others, initially I felt daunted by the task as this is my first book. Looking back, I had fun writing it and I hope you will enjoy reading it.

Introduction

Many people think that if you have a large piece of land you can easily set up a glampsite. Technically yes, but in reality this may not be the case. There are so many variables involved in setting up a glampsite, from doing your research first, finding out whether this really is what you want to do and why you want to do it, to whether it is legally and financially viable. Nowadays, glamping has become so popular within the UK, especially with promotion on television, that glampsites have shot up everywhere, and not just in the countryside, even in urban areas. As long as you have a large garden or green field, with planning permission it is possible to construct a small, quirky accommodation unit and rent it out to holidaymakers to earn some extra income.

Many glampsites start out with just one unit and develop over time with more accommodation. Even buying an existing glampsite resort with a number of accommodation units will bring new challenges that the owner will learn from. There are so many more areas that have to be considered than just the size of the site, such as facilities and where, when and how to build these facilities within legal requirements.

Like all businesses, there will be things you do that you will look back on as 'mistakes', but it is the learning from making the mistakes which is most valuable.

Setting up the business is only half the fun! The other half is marketing and promoting it; as they say, 'getting bums on seats'. After all, you are a business and rely on customers to book and enjoy their stay with you instead of your competitors, and there are many smart ways to achieve this. Your guests are VIPs in your business; without them you have no business, so getting the right balance between looking after your guests, and aiming to exceed their expectations is no mean feat!

This is a people business so expect praise as well as complaints; the key thing is to handle both well by having a professional and supportive team . Mastering bookings and sales to increasing more revenue is an ongoing challenge. But the biggest challenge of all, is to look after yourself to avoid burnout. Ultimately, as well as making sure your guests are happy, you should ensure you are too!

Chapter 1

Getting Started – Deciding why you want to set up a glampsite

Why do you want to do it?

This is an important question to ask yourself and especially to try and get to the hard core truth of what is motivating you to own and run your own glampsite.

Hard Facts to consider before embarking on the project.

Often we are fed up with our job, the weather, the hum drum of life. We dream of a better life somewhere else, usually in a lovely setting either in the countryside or by the sea, with nice weather. 'The grass is greener' certainly appeals, but this mindset can set you up to fail before you have even opened your glampsite. It is great to be positive and take risks, but there are no guarantees of business success, even if you tell yourself, 'I know it will be a great big challenge, and it will not be easy, but the rewards in the end will be worth it'.

This is so much more than building your dream home that you often see on TV programmes, because once your dream home is built you can finally sit back and relax and enjoy the fruits of your hard graft. But when you finally have your glampsite open, there is very little time to sit back and relax and enjoy it; it is constant hard work! This is the plain truth of running any hospitality business, whether it is a B&B, guesthouse, hotel or campsite. All require hard work, perseverance, tenacity, patience and a lot of energy.

Running any establishment such as these is not for the faint hearted. And if you also a run a cafe/restaurant alongside, it be prepared for very late nights and early mornings to provide the catering. I have heard many a person say 'What a dream it would be to open your own pub, so you get to sit and enjoy your favourite pint with your punters and mates.' But what people do not realise is the hard work that goes on behind the scenes in running that pub successfully: dealing with suppliers, ordering stock, changing barrels, relentless cleaning, dealing with drunken customers, fights, competition, unsociable hours and diminishing sales due to pockets being hit hard by a challenging economic climate. Luckily we rarely have had problems with drunken customers, nor had a fight to contend with, but we can relate to the other aspects.

If you see this as your golden retirement and a way of income for a pension, running the business in retirement years, be sure you are very fit and healthy. It is as physically demanding as running a farm. There will almost certainly be times when you pay someone else to help you especially where physical labour is concerned, e.g. gardening and building work.

You will never get rich running a glampsite. Rich as in financially rich. You will of course become rich in other ways, which will be discussed later. It is possible to earn a good living if you are prepared to invest heavily financially to create a high-end glampsite focusing on 'glamour', with beautiful sleeping areas, with high-quality en suite bathrooms and/or private kitchens/dining areas, expensive furniture and furnishings, and offering a 4 or 5-star 'boutique hotel'-style experience. This is entering the boutique hotel market with a heavy financial investment to boot.

Many glampsites start off with simple units and facilities and over time, with investment and expansion, aspire to this end as it will certainly bring in more revenue, because you can charge similar 4- or 5-star hotel prices; but when you are operating at this level in a hospitality business, the focus really is on customer service. The business side is key to enabling success. Highly trained staff will probably have to be paid, so expect a wage bill. It can then feel like you have 'sold out' to your original philosophy of a simple, sustainable, glampsite offering a slice of 'the good life' as you battle on, keeping the customers happy and balancing the books for a very demanding business. It is possible to strike the right balance that suits you, be it pottering around the vegetable garden or feeding the chickens, as well as running a successful business so you can live comfortably. It all depends on your expectations of 'living comfortably'.

This type of business is really suited for someone who enjoys a certain lifestyle, pertaining towards the more simple things in life such as: being outdoors; being close to nature; foraging; enjoying hearing the birds singing; accepting living alongside wild animals, including insects; gardening; growing vegetables, plants and trees; love of the countryside, rivers, hills and mountains; and enduring weather conditions. If you enjoy these things, then this lifestyle is for you.

The responsibility falls on your shoulders as you are the owner. Be prepared for many sleepless nights worrying about anything and everything about your business.

This is expected when you own your own glamping business (and many people would say *any* business), that you often end up breathing and sleeping your business 24/7.

Pros of running your own glampsite

- A healthy environment to live and work in.

- A great place to bring up a family.

- A quiet and relaxing environment.

- A lot of natural space, allowing pursuit of a sustainable lifestyle.

- An appealing environment – a space that attracts like-minded individuals who want to help, work or enjoy as a paid guest.

- A more unique and different holiday than the run-of-the-mill hotel experience.

- An opportunity to work from home, so no long commutes to work.

Cons of running your own glampsite

- You will never get rich financially speaking or certainly not quickly!

- You will need to have a surplus of funds either from savings or income as a means of assisting the project even when you have been open for at least 2 or 3 years, possibly up to 5 years or more.

- Most glampsites operate seasonally, usually spring and summer, and maybe through autumn. Our glampsite is open April to October. So expect the 'feast and famine' approach to working and saving money and enjoying it. When money is low during the winter, you will need to draw on the earnings from the summer or do other work to tide you over. It is possible to open all year round with wood-burning stoves keeping the tent canvas dry and people warm inside during the wet and cold months, but demand is much lower unless you are savvy in marketing and can appeal to winter cliental who enjoy camping in colder climates!

- You can only take a holiday when you close for the season (unless you have excellent managers that you can trust to operate the site while you are away).

- Expect a certain level of invasion of your privacy – staff or guests, calling or knocking on your door with a problem that needs dealing with now!

- People who perhaps are not 'your cup of tea' essentially are living in your home and in the ideal world you would never invite them to stay, but they are there as your guests and you have to smile, and count down the days when they leave.

- The challenge is to learn to 'switch off' from work so you can enjoy your leisure time, and this can be very difficult, but there are strategies that you can try.

Where are you now and where do you want to be?

The impact of running a glampsite on others that are close to you

The first part of this question 'Where are you now?' needs honest evaluation of everything in your life right now and what impact owning and running a glampsite will have on others connected to you.

If you have children you need to investigate schools nearby and consider how the children will make new friends and adapt to their new surroundings? If you have a partner you will need to consider whether they will be working with you running the glampsite or will they be doing other work or even both? The same applies to you: Will you be doing other work as well?

You need to consider your finances. If you are buying land within the same country that you work and live in, my best advice is to stay in your job as long as possible or ensure you have sufficient funds. It can take a year or much longer if you are starting from scratch to build a glampsite to be ready for paying guests.

It is best to come together as a team (your partner, family or anyone involved in the glampsite) and do a brainstorming session with a large A3 piece of paper. Write out a timeline starting where you are now (but if you can start with the ultimate goal and work backwards that is the ideal) as it will be a lot easier to see all the milestones from 'sell business', 'sell house', 'resign from job', to 'contact removal company' to 'arrive on site', 'project manage glampsite project' and 'opening day'. You will become a project manager just as you see on those TV programmes about building your dream house, and as always most people underestimate the time it takes to reach their goal and finance it.

There is also a connection with your emotional and mental health to your physical health. It is important that you feel in a good place and balanced, with plenty of energy to embark on this business.

Even buying a business that is already successfully operating will not be as plain sailing as you had initially thought. There will always be unforeseen problems that you had not calculated.

Ultimately, you are asking yourself what the big picture will look like for you in the future, which will include any loved ones (partner and dependants) involved living with you on the glampsite.

What support and resources do you need?

Financial considerations

You will need to consider financial support: your income(s), life savings, loans, investments; and whether you will have a business partner or someone who will be a sleeping business partner providing the initial financial support, and therefore who will be expecting a percentage of the profits. A wise guestimation would be to make a 3- to 5-year business plan.

Will you or your partner be working while creating and developing this project? If so will you work in your new place where the glampsite is proposed to be built or from another place or country? If both or one of you are working, then you may expect a delay in hitting milestones in your project on time.

It is easier to complete the project on time if both of you are available to be 100% focused on the project together. However, this has to be weighed up against what resources are available.

It might make more sense to have one of you working in your day job, which financially is very beneficial, while the other one continues working on creating the new business and does a lot of the operational work to save hiring others. It all depends on what your time frame is for setting up and opening the glampsite.

This could be within the next year or next season due to limited finances forcing to get it ready to open and trade as soon as possible.

When you are a foreigner in another country who cannot speak the native language, you are vulnerable to being scammed or paying over the odds for many services, products and bank loans, because you are not familiar with how things operate locally. My partner and I have both experienced this in Portugal. There seems to be a perception among some locals in Portugal that when you are a foreigner you must be an affluent tourist so they may charge you a different price to that of a local person.

Although useful to talk to other expatriates to learn from their experiences, it is good to befriend locals who can advise you on the going rate for things and how to go about doing them (or may even accompany you to ensure you do not get ripped off).

Also, you will feel happier within your community making friends and developing personal relationships which will help you integrate within the community more. You are more likely to want to learn the local language and by doing so you will find that day-to-day living becomes a lot easier and more pleasant.

GLAMPING AS A BUSINESS

Some people decide that their current situation of work and where they live is so bad that this option will seem rosier. It is easy to look at buying a piece of land through rose-coloured spectacles, but it is also important to consider an exit strategy should it all go wrong and you wish to sell and even repatriate if you move to another country.

For example, if it is financially advisable to keep a property in your home country and rent it out; you will receive an income and if you needed to move back you could. Of course positive emotional and mental support are equally important, and extra hands to help with the house move, then physical labour on the glampsite are welcome.

> We have found that the Algarve's primary industry is tourism, the medium to high season tends to be from April to November and low season during the winter months. It is possible to rent out accommodation all year round either as holiday lets or short or longer-term lets. But it is more than likely you will have to drop your prices considerably during these low-season months, as there is potentially a large supply of accommodation available and a very low demand. The Algarve could be an all-year-round destination for birdwatchers, hikers, walkers and other outdoor enthusiasts such as mountain bikers or cyclists. It offers more than beach holidays during the summer season.

If you cannot afford to pay many people, a good way to receive help is by a help-exchange situation, where you offer free food and somewhere decent to sleep in exchange for some work. There are websites where you can subscribe as a host seeking volunteers for a small fee, such as Help Exchange (www.helpx.net) and Workaway (www.workaway.info), as well as World Wide Opportunities on Organic Farms (www.WWoof.net).

Research

Where do you want to set up?

The first consideration is location, location, location! Glampsites should be in a nice open, quiet space in the countryside, preferably near local amenities such as shops, supermarkets, restaurants, cafes and bars. Attractions are also important, so consider the locality to museums, castles, galleries, parks, botanical gardens, rivers, beaches, mountains, lakes, theme park attractions, children's attractions, activities or a UNESCO World Heritage site, preferably within 15 minutes' drive or closer, with good transport links or otherwise accessible. Ideally, if the land is close to a beach, mountain, river or cultural city or sites, then you will attract tourists.

The surrounding area next to your land is important. If it is near or next to a national park or a forest /woods so much the better. If you find a beautiful large field with a lake, but it is next to sewage works, your guests will have the unfortunate displeasure of these smells.

We use composting and recycling to reduce our waste impact. We use solar power to heat some of our water. We are planning in the future to go off grid. We educate ourselves in the latest news about new techniques in organic farming and how to become more sustainable.

If you are looking to operate and uphold principles of sustainability, then you should consider your immediate surroundings and environment. For example, our toilet system drains into a natural reed bed. We have a natural well.

We grow a lot of our own vegetables organically and strive for permaculture through continuous learning, applying the principles and sharing ideas. We use ecological products that are kind to the environment, and we encourage workshops and retreats in permaculture and organically grown produce.

We are committed to conserving the natural habitat of the wildlife surrounding our glampsite and encourage sustainability towards our local neighbours. We are endeavouring to use low-tech and hi-tech alternative energy systems to further reduce our impact on the environment.

Local/surrounding Community

As well as looking at the piece of land and properties on it, research the local community such as your neighbours and local village/town nearby, and see if they share similar ideas/principles to you. Not everyone will be as enthusiastic as you might hope when it comes to living in a sustainable way, but if you explain how it will directly benefit them you could be surprised how positively they will respond to you.

Key characteristics of setting up on land

- Land that is naturally beautiful and interesting.

- Land that is next to a UNESCO site, national park or protected forest.

- Land that is next to or attached to an amenity such as a pub or farm.

- Land close to the sea or next to a natural swimming lake, lagoon or river.

- Land offering seclusion for accommodation units, with views of the countryside.

- Land close to tourist attractions, activities, restaurants etc.

Research your local competition

As part of your research into setting up and finding the right location to set up your glampsite, you need to research the local as well as the wider competition. You will get a good idea from start to finish what it feels like to be a guest with them and it will make you more discerning with regard to what you would do differently to them. Obviously you should not tell them what you want to do, as you might find that their reaction is not as positive as you had hoped if they see you as a threat to their business. In any case, it is best to keep quiet and just enjoy being their guest. If you can stay at as many glampsites as possible within your competition radius and make a list of good and bad points of each, you could get a feel for how you would like to stand out from the rest, and offer something different.

For example, we have found that we are one of the few glampsites in the Algarve offering self-catering facilities, i.e. private camp kitchens next to each accommodation unit; but we do not offer breakfast. Many other glampsites offer breakfast and some may offer a communal-style kitchen for all guests to use. Some glampsites may appeal more to families (they offer large accommodation units), others may be more couple focused. Of course it is possible to appeal to a wide variety of people to attract more customers.

We have a mixture of accommodation, from small units for two persons to larger family-sized units sleeping up to six people.

Some glampsites offer more comfortable and luxurious accommodation and facilities equivalent to a 4- or 5-star site and others will be more simple and basic but could be very enjoyable for a customer who enjoys a more rustic and close-to-nature experience. Once you have gathered your ideas from these experiences, the next step is to consider carefully how you are going to implement them.

In the case of buying a glampsite in a different country to where you live and therefore anticipating making the 'big move', you will have a lot to think about. Purchasing a new property or business is a huge investment, so it may be a good idea to consider renting a property in the area where you want to set up your glampsite, to get a feel for the place in all weathers and seasons.

Legal and professional advice

Obviously it makes sense to seek legal and professional advice such as establishing the boundaries of the site from your neighbours' land. There should be documentation in place to support this.

Also, a professional survey should be carried out by a qualified and registered surveyor to establish this important information and anything else that may not be evident in the paperwork.

It is a good idea to have your own accountant and lawyer, who can advise on the legal side of complying with the law with regard to buying land and setting up and running a business. In Portugal it is a mandatory requirement if you set up and run a business that you have an accountant and a lawyer.

We ensured that both our accountants and lawyers were registered professionals with good credentials. Obviously some countries will seem to have more bureaucracy than others in setting up a business, so the best advice is not to scrimp on paying the necessary people to assist you in providing sound advice or you could be sorry later down the line!

The British Chamber of Commerce, based in the UK, have offices in Portugal. They provide a business advisory body which offers information on businesses, interpreter and translator services, certification and notarisation of documents, marketing, promotion and mailing services. You can also join and become a member and this could be a useful way to network, make new friends or acquaintances, business contacts etc.

In Portugal, for example, there are other legal representatives at the Local Town Hall (known as the Camara) that have to be consulted. They can assist you in the process of obtaining a licence.

Depending on whether you are setting up your glampsite as a business from scratch and buying land with or without a property, or buying an existing glampsite business, there is a certain amount of red tape that will need to be tackled whichever country you are in.

Financial support and constraints

In a nutshell this means how you will find the money to pay for setting up the glampsite. If you need a bank loan then you will need a good business plan which shows good financial projections (how to write a good business plan will be discussed later). At this stage it is better for your financial projections to be more on the pessimistic than optimistic side.

Business grants

It may be possible to apply for a small-business grant. If you are within the European Union (EU), there is Eurofunding available. The EU Guide, which provides information on state and private grants throughout the EU has a website, www.grant-guide.com, you can research to see whether you could be eligible and meet the criteria for a national grant, within your country within the EU.

Buying off-plan

Buying off-plan means purchasing a property that is not already built, which often is associated with developments. There have been many problems associated with buying off-plan, such as the developer or builder going bankrupt before the property was finished. Legally builders or developers should provide an insurance policy which will protect the buyer should this happen.

Buying land

The first thing to do is consult the local authorities with regard to planning permission, as well as infrastructure plans for that area in the future.

Financing by buying an existing glampsite

If you are going to buy an existing business you need to really do a thorough check through all the business financial records and accounts to be sure you are buying a viable, successful business that is already in profit, preferably for the last 3 years.

The advantage of buying an already successful business is that the glampsite is already set up and operating, and the business side should be running smoothly and making profit. As it is established and with a good position in the market place, and having a good reputation, it will have built up a client base from guests that have stayed, hopefully repeat guests as well as recommendations and referrals.

It is relatively easy then to pick up the baton and modify, improve and expand the business to get it in an even better position profit wise or just create your stamp on it. If you wanted to seek a financial loan it may be easier when you already have evidence to prove that the business is already in a good financial position, making money etc. than presenting a new business plan to a new start-up business where there are only projections and no actual financial evidence.

You are essentially buying a property and business (unless you plan to do both separately and live separately from your glampsite; however, we recommend that you live nearby to your glampsite so it is easy to commute to and from, and that your guests/team can contact you easily).

We live just 1 acre away, up a hill, which gives us the advantage that we are far enough away geographically to feel we have our own private home away from our business. This psychological separation of home and business is important, even if it does not seem so at first, especially if you feel that you always love to welcome people into your home; eventually you can feel frazzled by the third knock on your front door while you are having dinner!

As in the UK, when buying a property you should always carry out a survey, and ensure that your solicitor or lawyer carries out the necessary checks to make sure that what you are buying is above board. There have been many cases in Portugal where people have bought properties, either residential or commercial, then they have found that they do not own the land but that somebody else does, there is no title to the property, it was built without planning permission and so the list goes on! For example, in Portugal the industry watch dog is IMOPPI (www.imoppi.pt), who pass on any formal complaints and information on misdealing estate agents etc. What is recommended therefore is to ensure that your lawyer carries out these checks:

- The title (escritura) of the property is satisfactory.

- The vendor or person selling the property actually owns it.

- If the property has any charges or outstanding fines that could be passed onto you.

- The property had passed all the legal requirements with regard to planning permission etc.

- Ensure all paperwork meets all legal requirements before contracts are signed and exchanged at the notary (public official ensures all documents are in order and witness the signature of the title deeds).

- The escritura is sent to the Land Registry to be registered and the appropriate fees paid.

Of course, alongside purchasing a property/business, if you are a foreigner then you will also need to complete a huge amount of paperwork and deal with administration. You will need to apply for a Foreigner Identity number (Fiscal number or NIF), residence card, work permit, if you are non-EU, identity cards, tax residency (depending on the amount of days you spend living in that country; in the case of Portugal, you are liable to pay Portuguese tax if you reside more than 183 days annually). It is always a good idea to meet and register with your local Consulate in the country you have just moved to and plan to set up a business etc.

Common mistakes when buying a property or land to build a glampsite:

- Buying a property that is difficult to sell for a range of reasons.

- Buying a property in a poor location that is not sought after by tourists.

- Failing to have a survey carried out.

- Grossly underestimating the time and costs for a building or renovation project.

- Failing to take full professional legal advice.

- Being over-optimistic about the income generated from the glampsite, especially in the early years.

- Buying a property with a large mortgage or loans and finding difficulty repaying the debt.

- Finding out whether any subrogation, in the case of Portugal, property debts, including mortgages, local taxes, community fees, are inherited from the previous owner.

Creating a business plan will assist you when you meet with bank managers, lawyers, accountants, solicitors, architects, project managers, other professional people and people working for local authorities. It will ensure that you have thought through all the details such as why you are doing it, (the mission and objectives), what you hope to achieve financially, but also intrinsically. It is a good reference to keep you focused and on track financially and operationally.

Creating a Business Plan – A Fictitious Example

Introduction

The glampsite is a charming glampsite located near Monchique in the Algarve, Southern Portugal. The valley is well known for its beauty and hiking possibilities. It will be set up jointly with Person A and Person B. It will be located next to Person A and Person B's home. Each of the units has their own private camp kitchen with dining area. The facility has a relaxing outdoor lounge for socialising, a patio terrace with outdoor BBQ and pizza oven, a yoga temple, a fishpond, chickens and a swimming pool on Person A and Person B's own 10 acres of land.

The Market

Within the hospitality industry, the glampsite will be competing with other glampsites within the area, although it is offering more facilities than others of its size. All of the units are brand new and are furnished with good quality, stylish furniture and furnishings in a picturesque, peaceful setting.

Objectives

The objectives of the glampsite for the first 3 years of operation include:

To create a glampsite whose primary goal is to meet and exceed customers' expectations.

The use of the glampsite by visitors every week from Spring to Autumn

To increase our number of clients by 10% per year through personal customer service.

To develop a sustainable business, surviving off its own cash flow.

Mission

The mission of the glampsite is to provide rustic glamping accommodation and facilities in comfort and style, with a close-to-nature experience. We exist to attract and maintain customers. When we adhere to this maxim, everything else will fall into place. Our services will exceed the expectations of our customers.

Company Summary

The glampsite start-up expenses include:

Home-office equipment, including: computer, copier, fax machine, extra telephone line, desk and filing cabinet.

Extra computer for the office with Internet access via Wi-Fi.

Website creation. Advertising/association dues for the local touristic association.

Renovating the land for planting of trees and plants, and vegetable growing.

Building and installing each glamping unit (sleeping, kitchen/dining area, outside area)

Company Ownership

The glampsite is jointly owned by Person A and Person B.

GLAMPING AS A BUSINESS

Projected Forecast	1st year	2nd year	3rd year
Sales	£90,401	£110,214	£115,454
Gross Margin	£18,080	£22,043	£23,091
Gross Margin (%)	20.00%	20.00%	20.00%
Operating Expenses	£72,321	£88,171	£92,363
Balance Sheet			
Current Assets			
Cash	£4,546	£5,252	£4,989
Other Current Assets	£0	£0	£0
Total Current Assets	£4,546	£5,252	£4,989
Long-term Assets			
Long-term Assets	£19,898	£21,112	£22,141
Accumulated Depreciation	£6,565	£7,887	£8,989
Total Long-term Assets	£13,333	£13,225	£13,152
Total Assets	£17,879	£18,477	£18,141

Current Liabilities			
Accounts Payable	£2,332	£3,252	£4,242
Current Borrowing	£0	£0	£0
Other Current Liabilities (interest free)	£0	£0	£0
Total Current Liabilities	£2,332	£3,252	£4,242
Long-term Liabilities	£4,000	£3,252	£2,858
Total Liabilities	£6,332	£6,504	£7,100
Paid-in Capital	£0	£0	£0
Retained Earnings	£11,547	£11,973	£11,041
Earnings	£0	£0	£0
Total Capital	£11,547	£11,973	£11,041
Total Capital and Liabilities	£17,879	£18,477	£18,141
Other Inputs			
Payment Days			

Market Analysis Summary

The market can be divided into two market segments, families and individuals.

The market has been segmented into two distinct groups.

Families: forecasted to contribute 67% of the dinner-time revenue.

Have 2.4 children

>£30,000 in household income

67% have an undergraduate degree

26% have graduate level coursework

Go out to eat 1.6 times a week

Enjoy camping holidays as a family or speciality lodging, or providing a unique experience

Couples: comprise 69% of the revenue.

Ages 19–47

Individual income average is £20,000

72% of the individuals over 23 have an undergraduate education

Eat out 2.3 times a week

Young professionals or students traveling that enjoy being outdoors, close to nature, enjoy camping and adventure travel or sport and alternative lifestyle interests such as holistic therapies.

Service Business Analysis

While the glampsite industry has its upswings and downturns, the variance is less than the economy itself. The peak season is July to September and the glampsite attracts excellent bookings from holidaymakers due to the location of the site and geography of the Algarve.

Competition and Buying Patterns

The glampsite competition is from a variety of local competitors.

Customers desiring to holiday at the glampsite typically take several different factors into consideration:

Location: peaceful and tranquil, near beaches and attractions

Convenience of self-catering and savings on meals

Quality: comfortable camping; sleeping on real beds with clean linen; nice furniture

Furnishings and units spaced out enough for privacy

Environment: relatively pollution-free air, natural gardens, trees

Facilities: high quality for a campsite

Strategy and Implementation Summary

The competitive edge consists of an experience focus (ensuring that the customer's experience is really enjoyable and relaxing) and offering a tranquil environment. This will be accomplished through a variety of ways to be detailed in the Marketing Strategy section. The glampsite sales strategy focuses to convert potential and first-time customers into long-term customers.

Competitive Edge

The importance of a positive experience

Marketing Strategy

The goal of the marketing strategy will be to raise awareness levels regarding the glampsite and its offerings and value. The message will be that the glampsite is a relaxing, unique, comfortable and healthy, close-to-nature experience.

Print media advertising: specialty travel and holistic health magazines, national newspapers

Flyers

Business cards

Specialty travel websites and websites advertising glampsites throughout Europe

Specialty guide books

Sales Strategy

The strategy of the sales effort will be to convert potential and first-time customers into long-term customers. This will be accomplished using several techniques.

Sales Forecast

Sales will be modest during the first few months but will grow incrementally.

Milestones

The glampsite has identified four milestones for the organization. The milestones were chosen to develop achievable yet lofty performance goals for us. The milestones were picked to be easy to measure. The following offers detailed information regarding the milestones.

Cleaner: housekeeping of all accommodation units, carrying out laundry tasks and cleaning of site

Gardener: organic vegetable and fruit growing, general flower gardening

Maintenance person: repairing, painting, carrying out any maintenance work as required

Financial Plan

Current Interest Rate: 2003, 2004 & 2005 is 10.00%

Long-term Interest Rate: 2003, 2004 & 2005 is 10.00%

Tax Rate: 2003, 2004 & 2005 is 30.00%

Sales Forecast

Sales will be modest during the first few months but will grow incrementally.

Milestones

The glampsite has identified four milestones for the organization. The milestones were chosen to develop achievable yet lofty performance goals for us. The milestones were picked to be easy to measure. The following offers detailed information regarding the milestones.

Management Summary

Persons A and B are the driving force behind the glampsite. Person A has qualifications and 20 years' experience within the hospitality industry, as well as building and horticultural experience. Person B received her undergraduate degree, a dual major of business and HR Management, and has many years of experience in Human Resource Management for various companies in London, with qualifications and some experience in hospitality such as waitressing, bar work and working in hotels, as well as qualifications and experience in holistic yoga, massage and well-being therapies. Person A: New site searches, build out project management, accounting, office administration.

Cash Sales

2003 - £80,597
2004 - £255,15
2005 - £475,163

Subtotal Cash Operations

2003 -£80,597
2004 -£255,156
2005 - £475,163

Sales Tax, VAT Received

2003, 2004, 2005 - £0

New Current Borrowing

2003 -£20,000
2004- £0
2005 -£0

Sales of Other Current Assets

2003, 2004 & 2005 - £0

Sales of Long-term Assets

2003, 2004, 2005 - £0

New Investment Received

2003, 2004, 2005 - £0

Subtotal Cash Received

2003 -£110,597
2004- £330,156
2005- £550,163

Bill Payments

2003 -£50,960
2004- £127,404
2005 - £242,199

Subtotal spent Ops

2003 -£97,510
2004 -£226,604
2005 -£389,999

Long-term Liabilities Repayment

2003- £0
2004 - £7,500
2005- £7,500

Purchase Other Current Assets

2003, 2004, 2005 - £0

Dividends

2003, 2004, 2005 - £0

Subtotal Cash Spent

2003 -£103,010
2004- £314,604
2005- £477,999

Net Cash Flow

2003 -£7,586
2004 - £15,552
2005 -£72,164

Cash Balance

2003- £12,57
2004- £14,367
2005 -£34,540

Chapter 2 – Setting Up the Site

Complying with regulations

When setting up a glampsite most people might think about what sort of accommodation they would like to stay in: whether it is a yurt, tipi, or bell tent, but that decision should come much later, after you have a plan of the site and received approval from various authorities. Whichever country you are in, you will need to meet legal regulations. Fire safety is mandatory, such as fitting fire extinguishers and fire blankets, and there should be a clearly marked fire-escape route and assembly point. Depending on the buildings, for example a cafe or restaurant, you will need extra fire protection that includes safety doors, safety glass and fire escapes.

GLAMPING AS A BUSINESS

Before committing to your site plan, which may have been drawn up by an architect, builder or by yourself, you should contact your local planning officer through the Town Hall or local authority. You will need to apply for planning permission if you are making structural changes to your property. There are certain conditions and allowances made for temporary structures such as tipis, yurts and tents, because they are easily assembled and disassembled and are not permanent structures, unlike buildings made of stone or other materials.

Within the UK and Portugal, temporary structures such as tipis will generally have less red tape to comply with than a permanent building such as a guesthouse or B&B. Another consideration is whether you will be changing your home to accommodate a business or commercial venture. This is known as 'Change of Use' and therefore your local planning officer and local authority need to be notified with regard to planning permission and complying with building regulations. For example, what are the parking arrangements and how many accommodation rooms/units will there be, and what impact this could cause on the environment and immediate surroundings, including your neighbours.

The other areas to consider are council tax and business rates. A local valuation officer will come to visit and tell you what you are most likely to pay.

Your local authority will advise on what you need to do to comply with placing official signs to advertise your business or showing directions to your location. For example, if your sign is illuminated, you will require permission from the local authorities (within the UK).

You also need to seek approval from the transport/highway department of your local authority with regard to directional signs.

Whichever country you choose to set up your glampsite, it is very important to find out what the local laws are with regard to complying with all building regulations.

Providing Access to the Site

The main road to the glampsite should be wide enough to allow at least two vehicles to pass safely or it should have passing bays. Also, consider any potential hazardous weather conditions such as heavy rain storms, snow, etc. at different times of the year that might prevent access to this road or to the site. In general, the road should be levelled off enough that any small car can drive down it safely and also consider larger vehicles such as caravans using the road.

Site Facilities

Safety and Accident Prevention

As a proprietor of a hospitality establishment, you have a 'duty of care' to safeguard your guests and staff or indeed anyone who is on site. Putting measures in place for the prevention of accidents is vital. This falls under Occupiers Liability Act. The Health and Safety Executive has information on how to take measures to prevent accidents, with a range of facilities such as swimming pools (discussed in more detail later under 'Swimming Pools').

Alot of awareness of potential hazards and the action taken

for the prevention of accidents is common sense, such as cable-tying loose wires and replacing worn-out carpet, and of course stairwells and kitchens are particularly hazardous places for fires. Also, consider overloaded sockets or faulty electrical items, and the issue of smoking inside or outside. We have a no-smoking policy inside, because most of our units are made of a cotton canvas and can catch fire easily; also this policy respects non-smokers and, in general, the law.

In Portugal, due to the widespread risk of forest fires, it is illegal to have a fire outside in a fire pit from May to October. Smoking is only permitted outdoors on the terraces of the chill-out area, with the expectation that guests extinguish their cigarettes in the ashtrays provided on the tables.

Providing fire safety information

We provide fire safety information such as how to use your fire blanket and fire extinguisher, and a Fire Action Notice map, explaining the fire exit route and assembly point, should a fire occur.

Of course with a glampsite, because of uneven ground or rough terrain, there will be areas which will be more of a challenge to make them comply with regulations such as those concerned with disabled access.

You will need to carry out a fire assessment which will indicate what areas are 'at risk' and measures to be taken to improve on fire safety. You should contact your local fire service to come and carry out an assessment and provide information and appropriate training. A useful website to help you carry out a risk assessment within the UK is www.communities.gov.uk/firesafety.

Emergency Access road to the site

Each country will have their own laws regarding emergency access. For example, the access road should be wide enough so an emergency vehicle can turn around when exiting the site. Contact your local fire authority about specific regulations

Installing appropriate drainage on site

Investigate what the local soil is like and how it copes under various types of weather conditions throughout the year. If it gets water logged consider where you would install appropriate drainage. Consider what types of soils will affect the drainage, such as clay. Consider the soil for establishing gardens, growing vegetables and planting fruit trees. In some places the soil may be very fertile and other places not as much. You may have to spend a lot of money bringing in new soil.

Existing gardens and layout of the land

Is the land flat or with hills and mounds? Consider the layout of the land and how it could accommodate units and facilities. Will you need to clear a lot of the land from obstacles such as trees? Employing a tractor, bulldozer and other heavy-duty equipment such as lawnmowers and trimmers is costly but necessary to prepare the ground for the glampsite. Of course you can purchase this equipment as a long-term investment if you or any of your team are trained in using it safely, or employ specialist gardeners and tradesmen at the appropriate times of the year to undertake the necessary work. We have a tractor and other specialist equipment, but we have also employed builders and gardeners and other trades people when our team does not have the time or skills to do the work.

On-site Parking

Is there a suitable area for parking for enough cars that is well connected to the access road? Can an emergency vehicle park? Consider lighting at night. Also consider closing some areas of parking or a separate car park for night arrivals in the dark where their bright car headlights could shine onto an accommodation unit such as a tent. Or if this is not possible, prior to guests arriving, ask them to dip their headlights when they are driving around the site for the consideration of other guests.

Water Supply on the site

If you are providing drinking water via a water supply on the site (this specifically applies to the UK, but it is necessary to consult the local authority in the country you are applying to), then it should be within 100 metres of the site drainage, and the Environmental Health Department will require you to have it tested for safety sanitation.

There should also be a separate water supply, whether mains or a bore hole, which should have a suitable facility for treating toilets at a chemical disposal point (CDP). A CDP and waste water point may need to be a sealed system or, if it is connected to the mains drain, then this will need approval from the local authority. In the UK, see this website: www.wras.co.uk, for information on an alternative water supply required to clean chemical toilets.

Dry Waste Disposal

Dry waste must be emptied and contained in a secure dustbin and placed at a collection point for access and emptied at least once a week. In Portugal the refuse collectors will not come to our site, so we go to the nearest local authority wheelie dustbins and dispose of the waste at least three times a week in low season and almost every day during high season.

Health and Hygiene – Food Hygiene Laws

If you are thinking of providing catering facilities such as food or drink, e.g. breakfast, in an EU country, then you will need to meet the Food Hygiene Laws. Contact the local authority 28 days prior to opening your catering facilities. The Environmental Health Department will give you the necessary paperwork to register. The Environment Officers can inspect your site without notice at any 'reasonable' time.

Food handling and safety practices

If you are dealing with meat then be especially aware of disease-causing viruses and bacteria, such as *E. coli*, *Salmonella* and *Listeria*, that can be contracted by touching raw meat or eating meat that has not been cooked well. It is important that whoever is leading and working in the kitchen should be trained in Health and Hygiene, have a Food Safety Certificate and keep up to date with any changes in law and practice. We have found it easier not to deal with meat, but to serve vegetarian food from our communal camp kitchen.

Electricity supply to the site

You will need to check the electricity supply. Is the site mains connected or off the grid?

If mains connected, is there sufficient electricity in place to accommodate the anticipated number of people? Where are the power cable lines and are they safe? If you are off grid, how will you provide power such as lights? The initial cost to set up enough solar panels is expensive but could be seen as a sustainable, ecological and worthwhile long-term investment for your business and private use; and you can sell back any excess to the local electricity supplier.

We have some solar panels and a lot of solar fairy lights, which we have found atmospheric at night and economical to run.

Emergency notices on site

We have an on-site notice board which informs visitors of what to do in an event of an emergency and also this information is supplemented in our welcome pack folder, which is in every accommodation unit.

Public Liability Insurance accident insurance

All businesses need Public Liability Insurance. Should there be any accident that occurs on your land, then you and anyone on your land are covered by this insurance should they wish to make any claims for injury to themselves or damage to their property.

Practical considerations when building your site

Any natural beauty within the site needs to be preserved. Trees, meadow areas, wild flowers, even old rotting logs have their place and provide habitat for the natural wildlife. If you have to use diggers or other heavy equipment, ensure you restrict use to a minimum. It is near-impossible to replace native plants once they have been dug up. Also, restrict the use of strimmers, as self-seeded trees or wild flowers add a special quality to the site.

When using landscapers and gardeners, try to get them on board with your vision by making them aware of special plants and areas that are of special interest to you. Discuss with them what your ethos is regarding the natural habitat and what you are hoping to achieve to maintain a sustainable ecological environment for your guests and natural wildlife to enjoy.

Some guests like to know about the site, plants, animals, birds and your family, so be prepared for a lot of hands-on work. We enjoy teaching volunteers, as many are very interested in learning about organic gardening. Some volunteers have a lot of theoretical knowledge, have studied courses in permaculture and would like an opportunity to put this into practice. We are always open to trying out different natural methods in gardening. It really is an ongoing learning process, teaching and learning from the volunteers' and our own mistakes.

A lot of what we have done in gardening has been experimental. Some years you can have a great harvest with certain vegetables and other years not so, and then you have to work out why and see what you can do differently for the following year to help promote a good harvest. We encourage our team of gardeners to label all plants at all stages of germination.

People are interested to see what is growing in the garden, so we try and take photos and put them up on the website blog. If you have any ongoing projects on site, some guests are even interested in getting involved, especially the youngest ones! We often have young children follow us around asking 'What tree is that?' 'Can I have a go watering the garden with the hose?' Even though we never ask or expect guests to 'muck in' and get involved, over the years we have had guests wanting to make a cake in our main camp kitchen from the fruit they picked from our trees, or a carpenter wanting to make a table from some reclaimed drift wood he found on site, and a lot of children in the garden planting.

It is wonderful for us to see our guests happily involved, and there is nothing more rewarding than having a guest who lives in a very urban environment say to us, 'You know what, although I live in an apartment in Amsterdam, when I get back I'm going to grow a lot of herbs on my balcony'; or when they say 'I'm going to get an allotment and grow my own vegetables'.

Before you plan your site, you need to spend a lot of time in different seasons to experience the different weather conditions. Our glampsite is located in Portugal near the high ground and green hills of Monchique, which has its own microclimate because of the higher altitude; it receives more rainfall than most other areas in the Algarve region.

Once you experience the various seasons, you will be in a good position to assess where the best plots should be placed for the best chance of plant, tree and vegetable growth. You will always have restrictions which will govern the best possible position for your plots. You need to take into consideration shade, light and wind direction. Other areas to think about are planting gardens around the facilities, accommodation and other areas which are frequented by guests.

> We would see passing clouds coming from Monchique and know rain is coming, or we might be lucky and it would just miss us and pass over. We have friends who live near Faro and will tell us that they have their own micro-climate and can grow species of plants successfully that we cannot or vice versa. It is very much a case of 'tried and tested', due to all these various factors, whether a plant will grow successfully or not. June to September is a major challenge for us in the garden. We have very little to no rain during these months, which our guests like but the countryside does not! We are restricted by the water available from our bore hole, so it is a great challenge for us to water the garden every day.

The practicalities of providing water to the gardens around the site such as those near the showers, toilets and water (irrigation) systems are important. For example, we have rose bushes growing near our shower block because we have the pipe outlets flowing onto the plants. This recycles the water used in the showers so that the plants can benefit and grow.

Creating privacy with trees, shrubs and plants is useful especially to separate accommodation units. Remember sound travels, especially in canvas dwellings, as we discovered with our tipis, being in a valley, so this needs to be thought about when planning the site.

Choosing the right accommodation

All traditional temporary structures were originally built using local materials and were transportable. They were built to cope with different climates. Tipis are not always practical in very cold climates, because it is very difficult to put a stove in with a flu to expel the smoke. It is possible to create a fire pit in the centre of the tipi so the smoke will rise to the top through the ventilated roof (as the Native American Indians did); however, in a glamping situation where you want to have a bed in the tipi, it is not practical to have a fire pit with a bed and other furniture.

Even if you slept on the floor with a sleeping bag, there is a huge fire risk to consider and a tarpaulin would be needed to cover the sleeping area. However, a Mongolian or Western-style yurt is designed so that a stove can be installed with a flu. Even so, in very hot climates, a yurt may not be suitable, because it can get very hot inside.

Our tipis are generally cooler inside than our yurt, because tipis are higher and have a conical shape, with good ventilation at the top. The yurt is a dome shape and has a lower ceiling, even though it does have a crown with a flap for ventilation; but the ventilation is not as good as in the tipis.

The yurt also has four layers of fabric material: an outer motif layer, the canvas layer, the a layer of felt and the inner cotton lining which makes the overall material a lot warmer than the tipis. Tipis have only two layers: the inner lining (ozane) and the external cotton fabric walls to catch any external rain water.

The bell tents have limited ventilation so are warm inside when the weather is cold. They are made from cotton canvas materials with a plastic groundsheet. They have a limited life expectancy because of being made from a light-weight canvas.

Local Building Methods

With the price of yurts and tipis rising all the time, there are many alternative building methods to be considered. Houses can be constructed from cob, hay bales, rammed earth or wood. Other types of suitable glamping accommodation include gypsy and Airstream caravans, tree houses, glass domes and even converted shipping containers. So the list goes on; these days there are many new ideas. UK television programmes such as George Clarke's *Amazing Spaces* have great examples of the variety of glamping accommodation available.

All of these can be a great alternative if you have cheap or free labour available. Use local materials wherever possible.

Depending on your skills and abilities, to create a plan and detailed scope of work, you can hire either an architect, builder or interior designer, or all three. Many designers work on projects that do not involve major structural work or additions, and also offer assistance with material and colour selections. Architects may take on a wide range of work, or work only on floor plans, and leave the details of the electrical plan, sanitary ware and kitchens to another designer or builder. It is also critical that you have a budget for your project and that you communicate this clearly to whoever you hire, so the design can align with what you are planning to invest.

Creating a schematic design usually involves a rough layout of the floor plan and some simple views of the exterior of the home if there is an external addition.

The builder can work from the schematic plan of the outside, a dimensioned floor-plan and some preliminary material selections so that the builder can provide estimates of cost of the materials and build of the project.

Do not underestimate the number of things that need to be selected, from doorknobs and windows to countertops and light fixtures. To really keep a handle on your project cost, it is best to select every last thing ahead of construction. This will allow your contractor to tell you the prices for what you would like and properly schedule material purchases based on lead times.

The architect or designer will finalize the details of the construction drawings and work with a structural engineer or builder on planning how the project will be built. At this point you can go shopping for what you need, for example the floor tiles.

Accommodation units

Which is best: Self-catering or Bed and Breakfast?

We offer self-catering for our guests by providing private camp kitchens next to each accommodation unit. Guests can enjoy having a basic kitchen equipped with a small fridge and gas rings, so they can store food, cook and dine alfresco style.

Self-catering – pros and cons

Pros

- The guests can buy their own food at the supermarket, giving them freedom of choice to cook the food they like.

- It is more cost effective being able to self-cater than being forced to eat out in restaurants all the time.

- It frees up more of your time, because you do not have to get up early and incur the extra expense and potential waste on making breakfast every morning.

Cons

- You have to pay for extra costs in utilities: electricity to run the fridges and buy gas bottles for cooking.

- You have to pay for extra costs in maintenance and cleaning.

Bed and breakfast pros and cons

Pros

- The guests enjoy the convenience of a nice, freshly prepared and cooked breakfast, saving them money and time (having to make breakfast or seek out a cafe or restaurant nearby).

- You do not incur the initial building costs of building private camp kitchens.

Cons

- You have to get up early to make breakfast every day or oversee that breakfast was made and served well.

- There can be a lot of food waste.

- People snatch extra bread rolls or pastries for later.

What Type of Units should you choose? Tipis, yurts, bell/safari tents etc.

There are so many types of specialty lodging that you can buy off the shelf or make yourself. For most people, when you ask them what they would probably expect to sleep in when staying on a glampsite, most would say they would be sleeping in a tipi, bell tent, safari tent or yurt. But now there are so many more types of lodging available including gypsy caravans, domes, tree houses and wooden huts only to name a few.

Top Tip

If you can source a good quality supplier within the same country, and if you can get someone to build something bespoke at a reasonable price for you or, if you have the creative and building know-how, then so much the better! Ideally your structure should be strong enough to withstand all the natural elements: wind, rain, storms and a lot of sun.

Your land, environment and other conditions will help you decide which kind of lodging will best suit your glampsite and also what your competition is offering. If many of the glampsites are only offering yurts, then you might want to stand out and offer something a little different. You can buy these structures from various websites throughout the world. Some structures can be designed to have a wood stove inside and electricity (on or off grid) as our units do. Yurts, which are a type of home or dwelling, originated in Central Asia (Mongolia) over 3000 years ago.

Top Tip

Remember all fabrics have a short life span, so you need to take care of them. The more your units are used, and then cleaned, repaired and cared for the better they will be looked after.

Traditional yurts consist of an expanding wooden circular frame carrying three to four layers of felt, which is usually made from yak hair.

The frame consists of one or more expanding lattice wall-sections, a door frame, bent roof poles and a crown. It can be dismantled within 2 hours and the parts carried compactly on camels or yaks to be rebuilt on another site. We have a Western-style yurt, which has wooden poles and cotton canvas, without the internal lattice wood effect. It is on a raised, wood-planked floor.

Our glampsite has North American style tipis. These were traditionally made of animal skins and wooden poles by the nomadic tribes of the Great Plains, in North America. The tipi is durable, provides warmth and comfort in winter, is cool in the heat of summer and is dry during heavy rains. Tipis could be disassembled and packed away quickly when a tribe decided to move and could be reconstructed quickly upon settling in a new area. Our tipis are, however, a modern version, made of a cotton canvas and are on a raised, wood-planked floor, to help keep the water and insects out.

Bell tents are also made from a cotton canvas with a waterproof coating and waterproof groundsheets.

They have a pole in the middle that holds up the canvas with guy ropes which attach to pegs in the ground.

You can easily come back to the yurt or tipi, which may have been empty for weeks, only to find it covered in black mould from poor ventilation, or lack of use, or damp from a lot of rain. So consider opening and closing times with respect to weather conditions. We open April to October because outside of these months it tends to rain a lot.

The canvas units can take some rain provided there is enough sun to dry them out. It is also very important to ensure that all the canvases are taken down and stored away fully dry, otherwise they will perish.

They should be stored in a dry, ventilated area. The canvas can be cleaned, but carefully, using anti-bacterial products, without acidic chemical products. It is best to check with the suppliers of the accommodation unit what advice is offered in terms of cleaning and care for the fabric. There is always the option to paint the canvas fabric with special paints that help protect the canvas and also provide a lot of colour. We had very talented volunteers who were artists and painted our tipis in the style and colour of native North American Indians. Many primitive and modern designs can look special at night when lit up from inside.

Pros and Cons of Different Glamping Accommodation

Tipis

Pros
- Quick and easy to construct small 5-metre units and relatively easy to construct larger units.

- Natural chimney due to conical shape is designed for expelling smoke from an open fire pit.

Cons

- Difficult to decorate internally due to sloping walls.

- Larger units moderately expensive to buy.

- The cotton canvas is perishable over a number of years and will need to be replaced and at quite a cost.

- Cotton canvases on the large tipis are heavy to lift and need a lot of manpower.

- Canvas must be dry when taking down and storing away or it will rot.

- Open fire pits are dangerous and should only be managed and used by professionals for commercial use, that is, shamanic courses.

- Woodstoves are a challenge to control and some hot air is lost rising out through the top.

Bell tents

Pros

- Quick and easy to put up and take down.

- Cheap to buy.

- Good when it rains.

- Many designs available.

Cons

- Very warm inside during hot summer months.

- Can tear quite easily, so ongoing repairs.

- Guy ropes need to be firmly staked into the ground to hold in place from strong winds.

Yurts

Pros

- Dome shape is an aesthetically pleasing design and different types are available, e.g. Mongolian and Western styles.

- Round ceiling has a hole with a flap designed to open to view stars in the night sky and provides extra air and light, but flap can be closed if there is rain.

- Excellent for installation of a wood stove.

Cons

- Warm inside during hot summer months.

- Moderately difficult to construct; needs a lot of manpower to lift canvas on frame on a Western-style yurt.

- The wooden frame can break and so will need repairing.

- Ceiling flap cannot withstand heavy rain.

Cottage

Pros

- Very easy to clean and easy to decorate and change bedding.

- Cool inside; pleasant temperature.

- Wood stove easy to install and manage or other types of heating can be installed, that is, electric or gas.

- Stays dry inside when it rains.

- Appeals to families with babies or elderly people, due to comfort.

Cons

- Not as quirky as other types of glamping accommodation and may not be as appealing or in demand.

- May feel more disconnected to the 'at one with nature' experience that camping gives.

Gypsy caravan

Pros

- Very mobile, so can be moved easily.

- Fitted compact units, good storage capacity and can

house good facilities, that is, kitchenette and bathroom.

- Can give the comfort of a cottage, but in a more quirky atmosphere.

- Can have them made in a bespoke way.

- Well insulated to withstand all weather conditions.

Cons
- Fairly expensive to buy new.

Airstream caravan

Pros
- Appealing retro 'cool' design interior and exterior; in demand.

- Comfortable design to sleep in.

- Easy to clean and decorate.

Cons
- Expensive to buy.

- May feel more disconnected to the 'at one with nature' experience that camping gives.

Wooden chalets/hut

Pros
- Natural wood fits in with natural surroundings and

can promote the log cabin hideaway feel in the countryside/forest.

- Not well insulated.

Cons
- Can sometimes feel cold in the winter Needs to be well maintained, including regular painting of interior or exterior of wood and repair of roof.

Any alternative building methods will have their unique problems, challenges and costs, so before deciding on which accommodation to buy, design and build, you should do your research, first taking into account your budget, the weather conditions, lifespan of the unit, general environment and what your competitors are providing by way of accommodation, as well as demand from customers.

Top Tip

Try and buy manmade soft furnishings over natural fabrics such as cotton and linen, because they tend to be more durable

---

Repairs of Canvas

It is a good idea to buy a commercial sewing machine or be able to use one or find someone local to you who can do the repair work for you. Copydex can provide a quick fix. Even glue guns or hand sewing with a needle and thread all work to help repair any small tears in the canvas.

Furniture and Furnishings

Expect to replenish the units every year with some new furniture and furnishings, as some will inevitably get damaged and will not be good enough to use the following year. Mould tends to form easier and quicker on cotton and linen than on viscose.

Furnishing the tipis can be awkward because they are a conical shape, so in essence you are losing some of the height of the room. Bell tents pose the same challenge, where you also lose some height, but as the canvas is quite thin, furniture must be placed away from the canvas or it can wear it away or pierce it, eventually making a hole. To a lesser extent the yurt, which is a dome shape, has more of an equal height.

It is easier to furnish the small cottage, as it has four walls, like you would see in a typical hotel room, and so we have windows with curtains and a wardrobe and other furniture that easily fits this type of space. We find the cottage the easiest out of all our units to clean and get ready on changeover days.

We wanted our guests to feel comfortable while they were sleeping in their units, so it was important to us that they have a proper bed with a frame, wood or metal, and a mattress, with nice freshly laundered linen, pillows, duvets, quilts, blankets etc. We provide electricity in each unit through powered outlet sockets, with bedside lamps. Extra sockets are available for phone charging, laptops, hair dryers etc. Occasional furniture such as bedside tables, small side tables, stools, trunks, chairs and a type of hanging wardrobe, as well as plenty of rugs makes for a relaxing and comfortable stay.

If you aim for a 'boutique'-style approach to each unit in terms of interior design, with small details like cushions on the bed and occasional chair matching the bed spreads or complimenting the rugs, it will be more pleasing on the eye for the guests. However, decoration is very subjective, as we found, with guests liking some interiors more than others.

It is also a good idea to consider how you will dress the outside of the unit, including the entrance and surrounds. For example, we always have a nice plant in a pot either side of the entrance, bunting, and solar-powered fairy lights to brighten and welcome the guest to their unit.

Of course, you have a budget for each unit, so my best advice is to write out an inventory of all the items you need to buy and write an approximate cost for each item so when you go to buy it you do not forget how much you have spent. It is very easy to get carried away in shops and realise that you have bought items that are either too expensive or inappropriate for the type of unit. Even scour markets, second-hand shops, antique or vintage shops for that interesting, elusive piece. You can buy old junk and, with a creative eye, restore it yourself or ask someone else to do it. We have found many guests have appreciated this philosophy of up cycling the old into the new. You do not want your accommodation unit to look like a lot of old junk thrown together. It is a bit of a challenge and requires skill to make the 'shabby chic' look right.

There are many books you can buy which will help to give you ideas, and it seems very in vogue, especially in glamping, to create a vintage, retro or shabby chic look. Even UK TV programmes can help inspire such as 'Kristy's Homemade Home' or 'Fill your house for free'. It does take some careful thought and a good eye for interior design to dress a unit with some old vintage pieces and new items.

You can of course employ an interior designer or someone with a good flair for design or decorating to assist you. Interior design and decoration is subjective and a matter of taste, so there will be some people who are not into the shabby chic style and may prefer modern design, so you just have to accept that you cannot please all the people all the time, but people will be able to see from the website the kind of style you are promoting and if it is not for them then hopefully they will go elsewhere.

We also have private camp kitchens, which are a basic structure of a corrugated iron roof with wooden poles and walls, bunting, solar fairy lights, electricity and a main light with switch. They are basically furnished with a small- or medium-sized fridge, gas rings to cook on, a work top and shelves, storage space for the kitchen utensils, crockery and cutlery, pots and pans etc., a table and chairs for dining alfresco, some garden furniture and a hammock to relax in.

Toilet and Bathroom Facilities

You will also need to consider how many accommodation units you plan to build to house the maximum capacity of people; this also includes any staff that may be using them, taking into consideration the facilities needed The other question to consider is whether to build conventional, flushing toilets or compost toilets.

Pros for compost toilets:

- When the land is not supported by a sewer system operated by local authority.

- Low running costs.

- Unable to afford to install a septic tank system.

- Fully supporting principles of being eco-friendly.

Cons for compost toilets:

- They require certain skills to maintain them regularly or they will smell.

- Many like the 'philosophy and intention' of compost toilets, but in reality some guests prefer using flushing toilets.

As mentioned earlier under Complying with Regulations, if you are building chemical-treated toilets then a CDP needs to be put in, in order to empty the chemically drained water within appropriate drainage.

We have flush toilets connected to two settling tanks that

then flow into a reed bed. We have seen tomatoes growing in the reed bed and often wonder where they came from, because we did not plant them!

Bathroom: Shower/bath facilities

Private or communal? Flush toilets or compost?

You can provide a combined shower and toilet block or separate them, especially if you are providing compost toilets.

We have a shower block which is separated into 'ladies' and 'gents', with their own private entrance, and two flush toilets with a wooden partition and wooden door and lock for each toilet, as well as two showers providing hot and cold water separated by a very high tiled wall and door with lock for each. There are so many designs that can be made for toilets and shower blocks, and providing bath tubs with overhead showers are possible as well as Jacuzzi-style baths, depending on your clientele and budget. Obviously, if you want to appeal to more 'high-end', 4- or 5-star clients, then it is necessary that you provide high-quality bathroom facilities as that is what is expected even by those that lean towards being 'eco-friendly'.

For example, some glampsites now will provide en suite bathroom facilities to the accommodation unit – inside/outside or next to the unit. This could be a compost toilet with a quirky outside rain-fed shower or a cast iron bath tub inside the accommodation unit or a more conventional flush toilet with a shower and/or bath.

Glamping, after all, for some people is maximising the comfort and indulging in style and luxury, but still wanting to experience that feeling of being close to nature. The more stylish and luxurious the facilities, the more you can charge.

Gardens throughout the site

At the very least the surrounding area should have some green, plants, trees and flowers to add interest to the accommodation units. When people are on holiday, the immediate surrounding area outside is as important as the room that they are sleeping in. People expect to enjoy the outside space on a glampsite and, for many people who enjoy being close to nature, looking out at the trees and countryside while relaxing in a chair munching on a sandwich is a real pleasure.

First impressions are very important, especially if you have people who arrive unannounced without making a reservation and wish to look around the site before committing to a booking.

As well as general gardens around the site, we also have a separate organic vegetable garden with fruit trees and a polytunnel, which is a type of greenhouse. We use it in the winter months when we start sowing organic seeds. As much as possible, we follow principles of permaculture. We ensure that the ground is prepared using animal manure without any chemical fertilisers or pesticides. Nothing beats growing, and picking your own fresh vegetables ready to cook that same day. Organically grown food not only tastes better, but also is healthier for you.

The gardens do not have to be as well manicured as you would expect to see in a nice hotel, because it is still a campsite and people expect a more natural and rustic feel to the outside space.

Having said that, a well thought-out garden with a mixture of trees, shrubs, plants, annual flowers and plants in pots is needed. Also, outside seating to relax and enjoy the surrounding area is a must.

Our glampsite has a chill-out terrace which overlooks the valley, and we also have a shaded area with sun loungers, picnic tables and hammocks for guests to enjoy relaxing by the swimming pool. Around our glampsite we have wooden benches made from reclaimed railway sleepers for guests to enjoy looking at the fish pond or up at the starry night sky.

Maintenance of site facilities

The facilities that you provide can make a big difference to someone's stay. It also can make you stand out from the other glampsites, which may only offer minimal, limited facilities.

Site facilities always need to be maintained and this can be costly in terms of human manpower, materials and resources to repair, protect, conserve and improve.

We carried out a survey asking our guests if they preferred a natural swimming pool akin to a small lake or a conventional-style, chlorine-treated swimming pool: 80% said they preferred to use a conventional pool. Many said they liked the idea of a natural pool, but in reality did not like the thought of frogs and other living things crawling up their legs whilst swimming! So they said if we had both they probably would only swim in the non-natural pool, but enjoy looking at the natural pool, much like looking at a lake or pond.

The swimming pool was designed with families in mind and, although we do not have a shallow end (the depth is 1.5 metres at all points), we have put in graduating steps going down into the pool from one side. We also have a fence around the whole pool, a gate with a handle and a key lock.

Providing Wi-Fi for guests to use throughout the site

Nowadays it seems many guests would prefer to stay somewhere offering Internet or Wi-Fi connection. People have smart phones, iPads and laptops which they would like to access through Wi-Fi. We provide free Wi-Fi throughout the whole site. When you live out in the country as we do, it is more difficult to receive an Internet or Wi-Fi connection than if you were in a town or city. It has taken us years to provide a good strong, consistent service at a financial cost. We see the value in paying and providing this service for our guests and ourselves for our personal and business use. Obviously, there are many providers offering different packages and deals.

Top Tip

If you can afford to have your pool heated, then so much the better, as many people look for heated pools, especially in Europe out of the hot summer months, such as in spring and autumn.

Swimming pools – Should you have one or not?

Having a swimming pool will be a big draw for many people, in particular families. But at the same time it can put some families off with babies and young children, because then they may feel they have to worry about their little ones (unless you build a fence with a locking gate, as we have done); or it may put off couples who imagine that the pool will be noisy, with children shouting and splashing.

Most children like swimming or splashing inside a swimming pool! An indoor pool is perfect for colder climates and means it can be used any time of the year, in any weather; an outdoor pool, especially a heated one, means it can be used most, if not all of the year, and an unheated one during the hotter summer months. The size, style and type of pool will obviously depend on your clientele. A natural pool or salt water pool is good for the skin and also ecological.

Of course chlorine swimming pools need to be kept clean on a daily basis, and will need a pool pump operating on a continual basis, so there is cost and labour involved.

There are many pool heating systems on the market, from very expensive to a cheaper, more basic system. You could install solar heating for your swimming pool. You could even make a basic system of plastic pipes that are connected to the pump nearby, receiving natural heat from the sun.

Whatever size and style of pool you choose will need to conform to local building regulations, so again it is a good idea to contact your local authority and find out what the current regulations are for building a swimming pool.

Children's Play Area – Facilities to keep the kids and parents happy

If you want to attract families, then it is a good idea to install a children's play area. Swings, climbing frames, slides and a small sandpit that has a cover (in order to keep the rain and animals out) are all popular with children.

We have a children's play area which is quite central to our facilities and located away from our accommodation units (near to the shower and toilet block, and sunny and shaded area, with sun loungers and hammocks and swimming pool).

It is in a safe place away from any roads.

We have many families stay with us throughout the whole season. Quite often you see parents and children enjoying a tour of the facilities, moving from the children's playground to the pool to then relaxing in the shaded area above. Also it is possible for parents to be up in the shaded area and look down and see their children play in the play area. We have a small slide, sand pit with buckets and spades, swings with a see-saw and a children's picnic bench with a 'Kids' Tent'.

You will also need to make it safe for the children to play,

70

so think about sand or wood chippings on the ground in case any children fall over, which often happens in a children's play area. On the other hand, a children's play area can put off couples seeking a quiet, 'kids-free zone' and they may choose an adults-only glampsite. We have a few units of accommodation which are tucked away in a quiet corner, away from the families, so we always recommend them to couples.

Communal Lounge and Terraces

Guests who come to a campsite or glampsite will expect a communal area to sit in, relax and eat. If you are providing breakfast or other meals, then it is essential you provide a covered eating area, with tables and chairs or picnic-style tables with benches. You will need to think about the size of the area in terms of maximum capacity of people. If you are only building four tipis or a similar glamping unit, there will be a maximum of 16 people to enjoy the space; if you do decide to expand and build a few more tipis, then it may be wise to have a chill-out area for a capacity of 25–30 people or more (including staff). This also gives you flexibility if you decide to hold wedding receptions or other functions, or open to the general public.

We have a 'chill-out lounge', which is a very simple but rustic outside structure with a roof, tables and chairs, and sofas for guests to enjoy relaxing, listening to the chilled-out tunes playing in the background or playing a board game, reading a book or playing cards. We do not have a TV available as we felt that this detracted from the back-to-nature experience that many of our guests are looking for, especially for children who are used to watching TV or playing on their Xbox. We do provide free Wi-Fi so we see people in there with their laptops, tablets and smart phones, but generally it is a space where families and friends can enjoy playing a good old-fashioned board game or just chat over a beer from the honesty-bar fridge.

We also have an outside terrace area with a BBQ and pizza oven, which is where we host communal BBQ and pizza nights, which are very popular for guests to meet up with other guests and have a drink and chat. We also allow the guests to use the BBQ when they want, and so these areas need to be cleaned every day and you need to factor in the cost for this labour.

Catering Facilities

> ### Top Tip
>
> You could write on a blackboard 'Tonight's Special', to entice the guests to eat on site instead of going outside.

If you are considering operating a cafe or restaurant, then you will need to ensure that the cooking and eating areas meet local regulations, even if you franchise out these facilities, you will be responsible overall. You can increase revenue from the sales of the food, but if you are only operating a very small glampsite of four accommodation units and you decide to employ a cook then you may not make enough in sales to pay their salary.

If you are going to offer catering facilities, you need to decide which is the most appropriate for your guests. For example, if you are going to provide private camp kitchens for self-catering, then there may not be much of an expectation for provision of a café, restaurant or meals. You could provide a welcome food hamper or breakfast pack and other food packs.

However, if you are providing breakfast from a kitchen near the communal eating area, then you may want to maximise potential profit by providing more meals; but, as discussed earlier under Complying with regulations, you need to ensure you have the right licence and certificates in Health and Hygiene, Food Safety and Fire Safety in order to provide meals in a safe and professional environment.

Operating a cafe or restaurant is a huge amount of work: sourcing good suppliers; buying supplies or waiting for your order to arrive, which should be as fresh as possible, on a very regular basis; and hiring the right staff. Supplying a simple breakfast is one thing, but running a restaurant is another challenge in itself. You have to get the right balance between providing a good menu which is well received and not being left with too much waste. You could offer a buffet, as is often the case for B&B, or a family-style menu of three or four dishes for people to choose from, where everyone sits down together and enjoys a communal-style meal. Advertising or communicating what food is available is necessary so that guests can confer with each other and decide if they want to eat at your place or choose one of many restaurants in the area.

We offer themed food nights such as 'create your own pizza' night, which encourages guests to come along and roll out their own pizza dough and put on their own toppings, then watch it being cooked in the outdoor wood-fire pizza oven. This is a unique experience and very popular with our guests, as are tapas and BBQ nights. So by offering these themed food events a few nights a week and advertising in advance, you can get a good idea of numbers so that you are not standing around in a cafe wondering if any guests are going to turn up. Obviously, if you are open to the general public then you should again have a licence that allows you to trade to the general public.

But of course you then need to also consider how many people could potentially be on site at one time and if you have the facilities to provide for this maximum number. If you are going to provide alcohol then you should have the appropriate licence to be able to serve alcohol. We do not have a conventional bar as such with a barperson serving alcohol, but instead we operate an honesty tab system, where we have a fridge stocked with beer, wine, water, juice, milk, chocolate milk and ice cream etc., and guests can help themselves to the fridge when they want to and record, by ticking the item on the paper provided, what they took. The day they check out they pay their bill.

On-site supermarket and shop

Providing food items for guests to buy

A lot of large campsites that provide cooking facilities traditionally have an on-site supermarket or shop that sells food and drink, as well as other items such as holiday stuff that tourists like to buy when they arrive at their destination. It certainly is convenient for the glam per to have an on-site supermarket, but in order to make a profit and ensure food items are sold before their sell-by date, you either need to provide a farm-style shop with organic produce and quality items such as locally made cheeses and milk, wine, beer and other more specialised items that can be purchased as gifts to take back home etc., or provide basic food items which are competitively priced such as bread, milk, butter, water, tea and coffee, biscuits, cakes, toilet paper, ham, chicken, cheese, eggs, tins and jars, etc. You cannot of course compete with the large supermarket chains in terms of price and choice of items, but the glampers will appreciate the convenience if they run out of milk or bread and have to go 5 km to the supermarket on their last day. We provide a guests' fridge stocked with basic items such as milk, butter, water, cheese, juice, bread, beer and wine etc. that guests can buy for their kitchens and pay at check-out, as part of the 'honesty tab system'.

Entertainment facilities

Activities for guests

Large campsites often provide a day programme of activities for adults and children such as water aerobics (aimed at women), water polo for the kids, archery for dad and kids, and so the list can go on. First of all you need to consider who your market is comprised of and what is the demographic of your guests: that includes age and typical interests. For example, we have found that, despite living very near to a golf course and providing information about the golf course, we rarely have any guests play golf.

You could provide a few entertainment facilities in the second year once you feel confident you have established who your customers are and what they like in the way of entertainment (you can send out questionnaires to prospective customers and ask them) and research your competition and see what they provide.

Obviously, if you want to provide evening entertainment such as a band or a show then a stage would need to be built and of course this comes with a lot of expense unless you are creative with upcycling or are a handy person with a drill!. You could work with partners from outside or very local that you can recommend to the guests if they ask for entertainment, so a reception area should be well stocked up with the leaflets, flyers, business cards of nearby attractions and entertainment.

Our entertainment facilities are tied up with the communal chill-out lounge and terrace. We do not have a stage as such, but a corner in the chill-out lounge where bands or artists have provided entertainment for our guests. We have a Yoga Temple, which has been a good space to host all kinds of workshops.

As we open during the warm months of the year in Portugal, April to October, we rarely receive enough rain to warrant providing an inside space for entertainment purposes, but if you are looking to open all year round through all types of weather conditions then it is essential that you provide an eating and entertaining space that is indoors.

Pond and Farm (livestock) animals

Pets living on site and allowing pets onto the site

We have domesticated pets, our friendly dog and four cats, but we also have ducks, chickens and a large pond of around 35 koi carp fish and a variety of migrating birds that live on our land and nearby forest. We also allow our neighbour who has goats to roam on our land.

We appeal therefore to animal lovers, birdwatchers and people who like the countryside or to visit farms. As we have many families staying with us, we have found that in general children love animals. Quite often it will be the first time that a child has seen or fed a chicken, especially if they live in towns or cities. We feel happy to pass on information and experience, especially when you hear stories that, when some children from urban backgrounds are quizzed about their food, they often reply that it comes from the supermarket and have no idea that it originated from a farm!

However, if people have allergies to dogs and cats, we ensure that our dog is kept away from them and up at our house, and our cats generally hang around our house because that is where they are fed. They can be seen to roam around the glampsite occasionally and, if guests show their kind appreciation by stroking one or two of our cats who are very 'people friendly', then we can certainly end up wondering where our cats have been for a few days!

We provide information about our animals on our website, so people can see whether they wish to stay at a place where there are animals; we have photos of them in the welcome information pack.

There is of course a cost to keeping farm animals: you will need to provide an area for them to live in, which is usually a shed or hutch with straw and a large water bowl, preferably fenced off to keep other animals out and stopping children from entering the area, as well as feeding and caring for them; and when you decide to go away for a holiday you will always need a house sitter or someone to look after your animals, especially your livestock.

If you want to build a pond, then it may require planning permission, depending on where you want to put it and its size. The pond can be as small or as big as you would like it to be, but do not underestimate the amount of cost and labour it can take to dig out a large pond and put in the appropriate lining, fill it up with water, and care for and maintain with aquatic plants and a pump. It can take a few years for a pond to 'establish' itself.

Health and Well-being

On-site spa services

Nowadays, many people look for extras such as spas, gyms, saunas, hot tubs, Jacuzzis and holistic treatments such as massage to help them relax and unwind during their holiday. These extras can be costly to build and administer because you will need someone to clean and operate them, as well as provide the services.

We do not have a spa, but a more simple approach to providing holistic therapies such as massage, either in the outdoor Yoga Temple or indoors in a treatment room within a building. Both have their advantages and disadvantages. If a guest requests full privacy, then conducting the treatment in the treatment room which has a door that can be closed, is decorated with candles and aromatherapy oils, next to a bathroom, a massage table draped with towels and there is electricity for music to be played to help create the appropriate environment for relaxation, as you would find in a spa.

Overall, it is easier for the therapist to conduct a treatment in these conditions, as they know they will not be interrupted when the door is closed and they have facilities at hand to support the treatment, so the therapist is guaranteed a peace of mind, knowing that the guest will find it easy to relax and a successful treatment should result. If a guest enjoys the feeling of being outside, the soft sound of the wind and birds singing, and being able to look across the valley (if they have their eyes open), then they can experience a treatment in the Yoga Temple.

From the therapist's point of view, it does not require a lot of cleaning compared with the treatment room. However, the massage table will need to be put up, taken down and put away afterwards. Also, there is the inconvenience of the lack of facilities such as a bathroom or hand basin, which you would find in a treatment room.

Some therapists have said that they enjoy giving the treatment outside more than inside, as they feel more connected to nature and able to centre themselves more easily.

However, some therapists have found it easier to be centred in the treatment room, as it is quiet and away from any potential distractions, even if they are natural. The costs of running the treatment room are higher than running the outdoor space such as the Yoga Temple. If the weather conditions are bad, for example if there is rain or it feels cold, the treatment room is obviously the better choice. It is, however, good to have the choice, for the therapist and the guest. All yoga and meditation takes place in the Yoga Temple, as is any other activity such as Tai Chi, and it is also free for guests to enjoy the space if they just want to sit and look out towards the valley or lie on the yoga mats. The downside with our Yoga Temple is that it is rustic, made from upcycling a lot of reclaimed wood etc. that has not fared well during some bad winter storms. We had to rebuild the Yoga Temple because of bad storms during one winter.

Building a gym and a spa is obviously costly and we have not found that glampers have wanted them. However, saunas are in demand, as are hot tubs and Jacuzzis. Many glampsites have built some very creative and impressive services, some of which are sustainable and affordable to build, but these can be expensive to run, so you may decide to charge a small fee for your guests to pay to use them.

Chapter 3 – Setting up the Business

Part one – Registering your business

Registering your business is one of the most important first steps you need to take in order to legally own and operate a glampsite business. Whichever country you are in, you will need to investigate the legal requirements for registering your business. Usually you will be required to seek advice from your local authority, lawyer and accountant about setting up legally and appropriately. In Portugal it is also useful to consult the Portuguese–UK Chamber of Commerce and Portuguese Trade Office and Centros de Formalides das Empresas.

In Portugal, before registering your business, you need to consider these steps:

a) Apply for a Foreigners Identification Number (NIF) Number. You do this at your local Finances Office.

b) Apply for a Residence Card.

c) Tax Residence – if you spend more than 183 days in any calendar year in Portugal.

Process for obtaining a Tourist Licence in Portugal

There is so much red tape in Portugal, where, when you speak to one lawyer or accountant for advice on obtaining the appropriate Tourist Licence, they will tell you something different, and the same can go for visiting different local authorities. So the following steps are a guide only; nothing relating to legal processes is clear in Portugal, especially the time frames. The law is continuously changing. So patience and perseverance are key:

1) The local authority office nearest to you can advise you with regard to the relevant requirements for your type of tourist business. If you are in need of a building permit, you will need to submit all architect and building plans to the local authority office.

2) The local authority will then consult with the Directorate General of Tourism (DGT) and Regional Coordinating Commission, and make a decision within 30 days. For granting permission for building permits, they may require further information, and a representative from the Council will visit the site to make an assessment.

3) Once the site has been built, it is necessary to apply for a Permit for Tourism Use. A representative from the council will visit and inspect the site. Visits from other legal organisations such as the fire brigade to assess for fire safety are also necessary.

4) After the Permit for Tourism Use has been issued by the local authority, there is a 2-month period

where the business owner waits for a final approval of classification, when a representative from the DGT will visit and inspect the site and assess for the final certificate classification.

Part two: Type of Business

Sole Trader

If you decide to set up as a Sole Trader and be self-employed because you are only running a very small establishment of one or two units, then this is a possibility. In Portugal, first of all you need a resident's permit, then apply to be self-employed with the tax authorities, who will register you with a tax number, tax card and a receipts book, in which payments should be recorded. For example, you have to pay into the social security system anything from 24% to 32%. It is possible to deduct business expenses from taxable income, but before claiming for these expenses they need to be checked by an accountant.

All businesses have to pay some form of a Company Tax, so you should find out what this is in the country or region you are in. In Portugal it is 25% on the profits of the companies covered by the general taxation regime. All companies must comply with The Company Act in Portugal and the Labour Law.

Private limited company

A private limited company has restrictions or limitations on its ownership with regard to its shareholders buying and selling their shares and also has protection from any hostile take-overs.

Our glampsite in Portugal is registered as an LDA. A Portuguese LDA comes from a private limited liability company in Portugal, also known as 'quota' or Sociedade por quotas de responsabilidade limitada. It is the most common type of business structure in Portugal, especially for small and medium-sized companies. As a registered LDA business, we have a list of businesses that we are allowed to officially trade as and amongst them a Tourist Rural for accommodation was one. A minimum share capital of €5,000 has to be provided in order to set up the company.

Public limited company

Being a Public Limited Company (PLC) means you can set up to sell shares and trade to the public on the stock market. This is obviously only if you are expecting to establish a large glampsite which will be successful enough to have shareholders and float on the stock market. In Portugal €50,000 is the minimum for shares, with a minimum of five shareholders.

Limited partnership (Sociedadeem Comandita – SC)

Limited Partnerships in Portugal are only formed between at least two partners, and no minimum capital is required. One partner has to be General Manager and have full liability for the company's obligations, while the other has limited liability.

General partnership (Sociedadeem Nome Collectivo – SNC)

General partnerships also have at least two partners, both fully responsible for the company's obligations, decisions and management. No minimum capital is required.

Buying a franchise

A franchise is where a glampsite business will grant a licence for a franchisee to trade under the same brand name ensuring they are following the brand concept, their policies, procedures and products. The franchiser has the ultimate control of operations. The franchisee has control of the day-to-day management and operation of the glampsite. This usually works well in a situation where there are a number of glampsites available to franchise under a large, central Head Office.

In the UK there are some large camping sites that offer this type of arrangement. They have made it appealing to land owners to run a small site, because they will make it easy to obtain a licence and grant planning permission on your behalf. There are low set-up costs, the organisation will assist in promoting and marketing the site and it is already well established in the camping community. However, franchisees can only be open to the organisation's club members and so potentially could lose out on other customers interested in staying.

Part three: Employer Responsibilities

Recruiting staff

When deciding to recruit staff to assist you, you will need to consider the various types of recruitment methods. You can recruit directly yourself by placing recruitment advertisements locally in newspapers, on the Internet via local forums or specialist websites and further afield abroad. When we recruited our managers we placed advertisements within the recruitment section of international campsite websites and also on our volunteer websites. So you never know how you will find the jewel in the crown, but choosing appropriate and varied recruitment methods will help you cast the net wide enough to find the best individuals for the job.

As with all recruitment, depending on which country you are in there will be employment laws that you will need to adhere to. For example, ensure you follow guidelines on good practice in order to refrain from discrimination towards prospective employees and to employees who are working with you.

We have volunteers who we recruit from various volunteer organisations' websites: WWOOF (World Wide Opportunities on Organic Farms), Workaway, and Help Exchange (HelpX). There is no official employment contract in place as it is not legally necessary, because volunteers are primarily on a working holiday. However, we do have a volunteer agreement whereby volunteers will carry out various duties for around 5 hours a day, with 2 days a week off, helping us in exchange for free accommodation and meals, usually for between 2 and 4 weeks' duration. We both sign to agree to the terms and conditions of work and accommodation/food. We employ a Manager(s) who lives on site and therefore receives free accommodation and free meals, and we pay them a salary.

Leadership and Management style

It is obviously important to try and develop good working relationships with your staff, to encourage a positive team-working environment where everyone can be open and commit to support each other to get the work done in a pleasant and enjoyable atmosphere. It cannot be expected that the business owner alone is fully responsible for the success of the business. That assumption can mean that you take on all tasks yourself and fail to delegate the work to the appropriate members of the team. This can create a feeling of disempowerment for your staff and you can end up feeling overburdened and exhausted. It is always a challenge to lead and manage staff effectively at the same time, because leading and managing are both different in style.

As Edgar Schein puts it: **'Leaders create and change cultures, while managers and administrators live with them.'**

Richard Branson is a great example of a very successful leader who has vision of the future and ability to communicate it, motivate, support, trust and constantly strive for improvement.

The manager's role focuses more on goal setting, planning, task management, discipline and procedures. Resources are in place to best enable the manager to do this, for example administration tasks such as schedules and timetables, and other time-management tools via various software applications.

When we hire our managers we expect them to take on the roles and responsibilities of a manager, working closely with the volunteers, training and supporting them as well as supervising the day-to-day work around the site. We are also present around the site in a supportive operational way alongside the managers. We have regular meetings with our team and managers, encouraging open dialogue and feedback. Having a happy, motivated team with the right skills will ensure that your guests are also happy. If you have an unhappy team member, they can outwardly display their negativity, thus creating an uncomfortable atmosphere for the team as well as the guests. It is important to tackle these issues or conflict immediately by having a chat with them to find out what you can do to support them so they can feel the issues are resolved and they can feel happy again.

Sometimes it works better for all concerned that the member of staff leaves rather than stays on, despite all your best efforts to support them. For example, we have challenges with volunteer loyalty and found that some volunteers start to get 'itchy feet' to travel or move on, and the best intention in the world to support them and give them what they want will still mean they are eager to leave and start a new adventure somewhere else. We have accepted this to be a characteristic of many volunteers and ask them to sign the volunteer agreement giving us at least one week's notice (preferably longer) so we can find another volunteer to replace them. Other examples are when some team members will not pull their weight, or they make repeated mistakes even after further training and support.

Training and Developing your team

Once you have recruited your team, it is important to consider how best to train them to get the best out of them to do the work. Our managers are responsible for the induction on the first day whereby they show the volunteer around and talk through their duties, with the aid of a written training manual of various daily tasks that need to be completed by the volunteer, and the Volunteer Agreement and their living arrangements. The next day the volunteer shadows the manager, who actively shows them how to carry out their daily tasks. Then they are assigned to work with a more experienced volunteer to help them carry out the tasks.

Employer's liability insurance

It is important to provide a safe and secure working

environment for all your workers. It is therefore your responsibility to ensure that you pay for Employer's Liability Insurance in case anyone on site has any accidents. Also, ensure you have adequate and appropriate insurance cover in other areas relating to theft, damage, personal injury as well as fire for your site, your property and people on your site.

Quality control

It is vital that you can assess the quality of the work being carried out via quality-control inspections by the management team. Our managers inspect the facilities and accommodation to ensure that they are always achieving the same consistent standard and, if it is not met, it is the responsibility of the manager to rectify it so it meets that standard. Customers have an expectation of quality and you want to ensure that you make every reasonable effort to meet this expectation. You do not want to wait for complaints from guests unhappy that their tipi was not very clean when they arrived!

Data Protection and Keeping records

As you will be receiving personal and confidential information from enquiries and guests who have stayed with you, it is your responsibility to ensure that this information is protected and held in confidential files, filed away securely. You will have data which will be in your business emails and also from your website and may be saved in databases. Also, you may have paper versions, such as booking forms or printouts of emails or spreadsheets which contain personal information. Under the law, we are expected to keep paper records for a minimum of 7 years.

Also, guests do not expect you to share their personal data with third parties, so this trust should not be broken.

Managing the budget

As with all businesses, monitoring a budget is crucial. Planning an annual budget, forecasting spend and having a contingency budget (unforeseen costs that arise) are all necessary. In the first year it is very difficult to be accurate, because you are very much in unknown territory.

Cash flow is important, and ensuring that you have good relationships with your banks and/or lenders is necessary when you may need to borrow money unexpectedly. Planning a budget and breaking it down in terms of fixed costs (such as rent, mortgage, loans, insurance and utility bills) and variable costs (salaries, stock, e.g. furniture and furnishings) is necessary. There are many finance planning tools available. Recording data in Excel spreadsheets is an effective way to track your budget spend. Your accountant will also be able to provide useful financial information for you, so it is a good idea to maintain a good relationship with your accountant, especially if you find it challenging maintaining financial records. By law you must keep financial records, especially for tax purposes.

Taxation and social security

Depending on the country, you will need to pay tax. This can be business tax, income tax and social security, as well as other taxes. It is best to consult a qualified accountant and lawyer about these complex issues, as we found here in Portugal. Here, as businesses are allowed to claim for a variety of expenses, it is important to keep relevant receipts, because, along with depreciation of assets, fixed and variable costs, and profits etc., your accountant will calculate what taxes you are expected to pay at the end of the tax year.

Consumer protection from unfair trading regulations 2008

This is the EU ruling whereby companies must not mislead or sell a product or service to a consumer. Be mindful of this Act and also, if you are in the UK, The Trade Descriptions Act (1968) with regard to all areas of your business from your website, advertising and information you provide to prospective guests (enquiries) and guests who stay with you. Of course this can be a subjective area, especially for guests who stay with you and then complain to you that they had a different expectation of the site, accommodation facilities or service and then request compensation. This is a challenging issue and one which should be handled carefully by listening to their feedback, recording and analysing it, taking it on board for the future (if they are constructive and reasonable complaints) for improving in those areas and negotiate compensation if you feel fair and appropriate.

Registration of guests

Once guests arrive it is mandatory to have a register of any guests on site. This is in case of an emergency. Also, within the UK, the law of the Immigration Hotel Record Order (1972) makes it necessary to record the name and nationality of all guests over 16 years old.

Sample registration form for guests

Name	Address	Car registration#	Nationality	Passport # Place of issue	Arrival Date	Depart date

Part Four A: Advertising Your Business

Establishing your brand and logo

As with all successful businesses, the brand and logo make a big impact on the public. People remember the name easily (if it rolls off the tongue), what the business is selling, and imagine what it looks like just from the logo. So it is a good idea to spend some time thinking about who you are, what you are about and who you are trying to attract so that you can captivate your audience.

Before arriving at the name of your business, just like musicians thinking of a suitable band name, it will require brainstorming ideas and coming up with a number of names and looking for one that is the most original. You should look at other names of similar businesses, so you do not choose the name of somebody else and get into hot water with copyrights and patents; therefore it is beneficial to do some research.

Once you have chosen the name of your business, turn to how you will present your name, think about the overall image, picture and text, and colour which will convey the message of a glamping site. This logo should be consistently used throughout your business: on your website, on brochures, business cards and signs. Later on, you can use your logo in marketing and promotional material to continue to establish your brand. We created postcards which we left in our chill-out lounge for guests to send home to friends and family and had T-shirts printed with our logo.

Using the Internet – Websites: your own and others

Nowadays, most people who are looking to go on holiday will use the Internet to search for what they desire. It is beneficial to advertise on specific niche websites offering glamping or camping holidays, or even just alternative holidays.

The best way to find out what are the most appropriate websites to advertise on is by doing a Google search with a variety of key words such as 'Glamping holidays, Portugal' or ' Tipi Holidays, Algarve', then on page 1 of Google you will see a list of websites to choose from relating to your search.

Usually this will include other competitors (so it is good to see how high they rank in Google and reach out to potential customers) and websites advertising glamping holidays. We chose to advertise with some of these websites, because of their ranking in Google and because people like to have a choice of places to look at before deciding where they want to go. But of course in order to advertise on these websites you must have a website yourself!

Creating your own Website

We have seen the value in providing a professional-looking website with regularly updated information, including photos, pricing and promotional offers. Also, it is highly likely that people searching for a glamping holiday will also look at other websites and, if yours looks outdated (e.g. circa 1995), then they may just click off it after a few seconds, not giving you a chance. Years ago it was easy to visit a web designer with marketing brochures and other marketing materials and expect them to create a website. Nowadays, expectations from viewers are much higher and so now websites are designed around objectives, needs, wants, expectations from the target audience, products and services offered. Other factors that should be considered also: it should be search-engine friendly, encourage repeat visitors; and encourage customer loyalty through exclusive discounts or having a members-only forum or have interactive tools such as virtual tours and interactive maps.

Plan your website design to include:

- Content guidelines
- Text guidelines
- Colour guidelines
- Navigation guidelines
- Graphic guidelines
- Visual guidelines

The average duration people will spend looking at a website can just be a couple of minutes (they can of course return again and again) so you want to try and you're your visitors into customers. Your home page is key to displaying the most vital information about your glampsite and be 'value-added' by speaking directly to your target viewer, summarising the most important points about your glampsite such as accommodation and facilities, with excellent high-resolution photos and a Banner Ad (moving images or photos that can be rotated in a specific order, so you can have a number of photos of your site on the home page) to support this content. It is worth breaking down who your target viewers are: holiday travellers, couples, groups or families, and by country.

Also, consider business travellers, tour operators, advertising websites, outdoor-activity operators, retreat leaders and wedding planners; the list can go on and on! Are you meeting the needs, wants and expectations of all these type of website viewers?

A website is a useful marketing tool as well and can be used to produce e-brochures and i-brochures. These are electronic versions of the paper brochures and contain all the information you want your target market to read. An i-brochure is set up with a macromedia flash with a page-turning facility, just as you would turn pages with a paper brochure, so it is complementary to your website. It is cheaper having an i-brochure facility available then posting out paper brochures to your prospective customers. Also, virtual postcards are another effective way to reach out to people via an email, which could be forwarded on to friends and family.

It is worth looking into audio and video, for example creating a video of your glampsite and have that displayed on the home page of your website. You could hire a professional photographer/technical person or create one yourself. A certain feeling can be created which is difficult to obtain just through website text, so people can get a sense of what the place may look and feel like, and what experiences they might have staying with you. 'A picture can tell a thousand words' after all!

It is worth the initial start-up costs of hiring a web designer, which can be anything from 1,000 to €5,000 (which I highly recommend, unless you are very creative or web savvy and can design and execute your own professional-looking website). Another reason for people choosing their holiday is because they like the website, think it is easy to navigate through, the photos are clear and all their questions are answered via the information contained within it, but for unanswered questions they can contact someone for further information. Plus, it is easy to book or reserve accommodation if they wish to. You could have an availability calendar on your website so people can view what accommodation (photos and descriptions of the unit) is available, the dates it is available and the price for that duration. A lot of people are lacking time and want to book immediately, so this tool allows them to do so.

It is vital you have great content which is eye catching, clear, concise and gives the 'wow' factor, so it must be tailored to the viewer. The text tells the viewer that you are providing a certain service and should captivate them to want to continue reading and ultimately make an enquiry to book accommodation!

Creating a Blog

It is useful to create a blog that is linked to your website. You can set up a blog using free blog-hosting sites such as Blogger.com or by using software packages such as http://wordpress.org, or you can create your own blog using HTML.

You can add additional information, such as photos of guests having a good time, or promote upcoming events/workshops and discounts with more detail than if you mention it on your website. Blogs can be used to provide potential and existing customers with the latest news of what is going on at your glampsite. Using key words in your subject headings and content specifically relating to glamping searches will help your search engine placement; for example, glamping fun in the sun in the Algarve, Portugal. Google Key Word searches for glamping in Portugal: glamping, Algarve, Portugal, etc.

Blogging (writing the content of a blog) is also very user friendly; most people who do not consider themselves very 'technical' and would not feel comfortable updating a website could happily edit a blog. Each article you add is called a blog post and you can easily upload photos or pictures to it. Blogs focus on a subject area or topic, for example: 'Little glampers enjoying feeding the ducks and chickens!' You can have an RSS (Really Simple Syndication) feed, which is basically a delivery channel through which you can send content to subscribers and other websites.

Blogs do need updating regularly so they appear current, which does take up time.

Before creating a blog, you should do some research and look at the wide variety of blogs available on the Internet for inspiration regarding style, content etc. Focus on blogs relating to hotels and hospitality, and of course more specifically campsites and glampsites. You can use search engines such as Google, Blog Search, and Blogorama.

Marketing via emailing: Newsletters

Using email is crucial to stay connected to existing and encourage prospective customers to contact you. We use Gmail as an email provider as we have found it a good, user-friendly and secure email site. On the Contact Us page on our website, as well as a contact form that the website viewer must complete in order to contact us, we give them the option to contact us directly using our company Gmail address. At this point, whichever method they used to contact us, they will automatically receive an email (called an auto responder) which states 'Thank you for contacting us, we will endeavour to respond within 48 hours.' Once you receive an enquiry, you already have an email address which is very useful for marketing purposes. You can save this email and it can be used on a mailing list and to email out newsletters and i-brochures at a later date. Every marketing email sent must give the recipient the option to unsubscribe every time.

We send out newsletters three or four times a year, usually starting in the winter, wishing everyone a Happy New Year and highlighting the projects to take place to help improve the glampsite, plus special offers and promotions for the opening of the new season in spring. Another newsletter goes out about 2 months later, showing the progress of the projects and maintenance of the site, with special offers and promotions. A 'We are now open' newsletter is next, with photos of the newly opened site, with promotional offers and discounts, then finally a mid-season newsletter mentions upcoming events, and other promotional offers and discounts. Some people email out newsletters every week; it depends on what suits you and your target customers.

As we do not run many workshops/events until our high season (July and August), we do not feel that it is important to email out newsletters very frequently, plus it takes time and effort. Also, we appreciate that people receive a lot of unsolicited emails and we do not want them to feel like we are pestering or boring them.

We feel our blog can offer a supplementary service of current information and photos, and we always mention our website and blog with links in our newsletters so that these email subscribers can investigate further if they wish. It is important to build a database of emails which can be broken down in terms of: enquiries, previous guests; friends and family; staff; external business partners etc., as you may want to send out specific mail to these groups.

You can use mail-list management software such as Mail chimp which does cost, but may be worth the expenditure because it allows you to easily remove or add subscribers. They have Spam checking to give your email the best chance that it will not land in the client's Spam box instead of their inbox, and a lot of useful, fast features such as auto responders built in, filtering, reporting and tracking.

Mobile marketing

Nowadays many people use mobile devices, such as mobile phones, tablets, iPads and smart phones to connect to the Internet and other apps. Your website should have the facility for your web viewers to view it from such a device as it may be the only way they connect to the Internet. Many marketing opportunities are available through this medium. It allows direct, personal communication in real time with the opportunity for immediate, direct response. You can enhance your brand and increase customer loyalty via targeting special promotions and potential increase in sales.

MMS (multimedia messaging service) enables audio, video, picture and text files to be sent to a mobile phone; SMS (short messaging service) enables sending out a text message to mobile phones, highlighting special offers and discounts. Instant messaging allows the mobile user to instant message and send and receive, mobile blogging – within an instant, videos, pictures and audio files can be added to a mobile device.

Objectives of effective advertising

Before considering what type of media to use, you need to understand how to write an effective advertisement. When creating any advertisement there are rules that professional advertisers follow.

You need to have clear objectives, that is: Who is your target audience? Where are they? What do you want their reaction to be? Finally, what will be the outcome or result of the advertisement?

You can use the AIDA rules:

ATTENTION – Get your target audience's attention through a compelling headline.

INTEREST – Stimulate their interest by explaining the benefits.

DESIRE – Offer incentives, testimonials from previous guests who have stayed and recommended the site, and so making this place is very desirable.

ACTION – Be direct and clearly state what you want the reader to do next, for example visit your website for more offers and discounts. But be sure to always have your offers and discounts continually updated (delete past discounts in order to avoid confusion). It does not look good if you are still advertising a Spring Offer during summer.

> Our glampsite was listed in the 'Top ten affordable family holidays for Europe, 2015' by the UK Guardian National Newspaper which helped to generate a lot of enquiries, so it can be a great blessing when journalists contact you to feature you in an article.

Part Four B: Using various Media for Advertising

Newspapers and magazines

On-line and offline publicity is the best way to achieve the best marketing results and bring new customers to your glampsite. Having a positive article written and published about your glampsite is more advantageous than paid advertisements. A journalist reporting will generally be seen as more unbiased and therefore more credibility. However, often you will not be shown the proofs of the article before its published and there is a chance that they may print something inaccurate or what you perceive as negative.

You can email various media such as magazines and newspapers with a Press Release, with a 'pitch', one punchy page explaining who you are, what you are doing, why you decided to do it, where you are located, when you are open and any promotional offers. Try not to sound as if you are reading from a script. If you have any relevant statistics such as surveys, then include them. It is best to send a pitch first, followed by a Press Release. A Press Release needs to be newsworthy in order to catch a journalist's attention; 250 words maximum, preferably on one page, and self-contained, so it could be easily lifted into an article immediately.

If you write it in the style of their publication you will appeal more. Explain which photos are available; no need to email unless they ask. Always follow up quickly after asking whether the publisher received it and whether they need any more information. There is a very small chance that you will get it published for free.

> One year we paid a lot for a very tiny one-off advertisement in the print version and online UK national Sunday Mail newspaper. We did not receive one enquiry!

You could create a press pack which will give journalists quick access to background information about your glampsite, such as its history, where you are located, your accommodation and facilities, and what is especially unique, backed up by any statistics. Include a profile of the owners and any significant members of the team such as manager and chef. Also, provide professionally taken, high-resolution photos (or at least ones that look like they could be).

Quite often you will receive emails from journalists wishing to speak with you because they are writing a glamping piece and would like to include you in it. In some countries glamping is still quite unknown or relatively new to the public so it makes a newsworthy article.

The UK was one of the first countries in which glamping

emerged, many years ago; whereas in Portugal it is been in the last 2 years that glamping has really taken off as a holiday for Portuguese people. Most of our articles that have been published by various newspapers and magazines in Portugal, the UK and Germany have come about because journalists contacted us.

Paid advertisements, however, have the advantage that you have more control over the proofs. Usually they will be emailed to you and you will be asked if all the information is correct; if not you can amend it. Some journalists will offer to write an 'advertorial' (which might be free if you are lucky!), recommending your glampsite for a holiday and at the end it will include your website details and promotions or discounts.

It is trial and error whether it pays to advertise or not in a certain publication. And yet we can pay a modest amount to advertise in *The Spark* newspaper, which is based in the South West of England and appeals to people who enjoy 'alternative' lifestyle such as complimentary therapies and holidays. We also tried advertising with a very specialist magazine called *Kindred Spirit*, which has a section on alternative holidays, but we received very few enquiries.

Top Tip

It is trial and error what advertising and marketing works. The key is to make a record of all advertising in a table with its success rate so you can know for the future where not to pay to advertise. When we had an advert placed in a local magazine in the Algarve, we received a lot of phone calls from locals who wanted to see what a tipi was (with no intention to stay), so it's important to strike a good balance when welcoming outside visitors for a general tour regarding your personal time, the safety and security of your site, and privacy of your guests.

We did, however, receive some enquiries through *UK Camping and Caravan* magazine.

Radio and TV

There is of course radio (local and national), which is traditionally an expensive way to advertise. However, you could contact regional radio stations, who may be willing to advertise for free if you come on their radio show and promote your glampsite. If you would like to run a small advert that they play during breaks, usually this has to be paid for.

TV advertising is the most expensive way to advertise and, unless you have a very large advertising budget to allow for this, it is out of reach for most glampsite owners.

On-line Advertisers

We had a lot of success by advertising with various on-line websites promoting glamping, camping or 'Alternative' or 'Eco-conscious' holidays. We found many advertisers through on-line Internet searching, but only if they appeared on page 1 of Google or another popular search engine. Some websites also contacted us, especially new websites which were not established and were looking for glamping sites that were already established in Google searches. They offered a free trial for a certain period of time in exchange for a link to our website. This seems a fair exchange, but not when they insist on it being on your Home page! It is better to negotiate with them to place their website link on a less important website page that fewer viewers will look at. It can take quite a lot of time to ing and fro ing between the advertising website and yourself to get your profile correct; but this is crucial as you do not want to potentially mislead any customers who may see conflicting information on your website and then another website you have advertised on. We had one website mix up our name with another glampsite with a similar name in Portugal. It caused a lot of confusion for the viewers, the other glampsite and us!

Internet advertising with Social Media

Internet advertising using social media such as Facebook offers a pay-per-click service This can be an effective way to generate positive responses to your advertisement. They are easy to track and see how many responses you receive, so you can gauge quite quickly whether this is an appropriate advertising campaign or not, then you can set limits on the advertising cost. When I tried to attract people to attend a yoga retreat, I ran an advert through Facebook pay-per-click. I did not receive many clicks, nor did anyone who enquired mention that they saw the advert, so I cancelled it and spent time and money advertising within yoga websites and received many more enquiries.

Beware also that anyone can just click on your advert, making you pay, so Internet fraudsters can indulge in doing this, and you have no real way of knowing if they are genuinely interested, clicking to learn about what you are offering, or if they have other intentions. You also need to monitor the clicks very regularly, because if you forget and it is popular you could receive a high bill, which is usually debited from your bank card!

Brochures/leaflets/Flyers/posters

There are also the more traditional forms of advertising via paying to print brochures, leaflets, flyers or booklets which you can distribute in various tourist offices or bars and restaurants in your local area or further afield or ask friends who live in different places to put up on a notice board at work or in their local library or newsagent's window. Take care in the production so that the overall finish looks professional (not typed on your computer and printed off at home).

We always have our brochures and leaflets professionally designed and printed, and there are so many suppliers out there offering competitive prices. Of course be extra careful when proofreading before it goes to print. You do not want 10,000 brochures printed with the wrong website address! Grabbing the attention of people is key to its success (follow the AIDA principles). You could have brochures which promote and advertise your glampsite overall or you could break it down by type of customer or leisure facilities. For example, if you have a spa or have holistic therapies on offer, you could design a brochure specifically informing your guests about these services. If your glampsite is available for hire for weddings, you could design a brochure aimed at wedding guests. Only produce specialised brochures if you feel that there is enough demand for this service to justify the cost of production. If your budget is small and you can have all these areas covered in one larger brochure, then this will save on costs (and it also means that they do not have to pick up five different brochures).

Tourist companies/information offices

You may receive sales calls from tourist companies to see if you would like to advertise within their brochure or tourist map. Do not be pushed into advertising with them; do some research first. We found that most of our customers have come from other regions of Portugal and abroad, not locally. It may be beneficial to visit all the tourist information offices in your local area and beyond, to ask what the arrangement is for leaving any company literature with them to attract off-chance bookings. Nowadays, there are many intrepid travellers who are armed with a guide book and happy to travel from town to town, who like to visit the local tourist office for extra information or advice as to where to stay.

> ## Top Tip
>
> Advertisements placed on the right-hand page in newspapers or magazines sell more because most people's eyes are drawn to the right side.

The advantage with a glampsite is that it is different to the standard hotel or B&B and will stand out and will probably be remembered by the staff working there.

Guide books

There are a lot of guidebooks available which you could pay to advertise in or, if you are lucky, could receive a free mention, as we found out from one Irish guest when they said they saw us recommended in the Marco Polo guidebook. A lot of glampsites would like guide books such as those by Lonely Planet to give them a positive review. It is possible to contact them and ask when they may come to visit and write a review, but they are often inundated with similar requests and you may have to wait for them to contact you or they may even just turn up anonymously one day and write a secret review. You can try networking by attending various groups and events, for example having a stand at a glamping or camping show such as the Camping and Caravan Show. This could be expensive, but your efforts and time may be worth it, as you spread the good word about your site, and you may receive some enquiries, make sales and meet other useful contacts.

Word of mouth

Receiving recommendations by word of mouth is the best

(and free) form of advertising. It shows you are doing something right and it is genuine. It is very rewarding and satisfying when you receive an email saying, for example, 'My sister came to your glampsite last summer with her family and they all had a great time and recommended you to me'.

What not to do

One thing not to do is follow what your competitors do with their advertising. It may work for them but not for you. Following the herd, or doing what is currently 'in' or fashionable can produce disastrous results. An example is a journalist from a national paper trying to seduce you into spending on a large page spread as part of their campaign, where they are desperate to get their sales space filled so they offer you a big discount. I receive so many phone calls every year from journalists or sales people working on glamping campaigns asking if I would be interested in spending X amount in their newspaper or magazine. One year I spent a lot of money with one magazine when I felt 'pushed' by the journalists to participate and it didn't generate one enquiry. Advertising can be expensive, so be wise when you spend your money.

Also, in marketing terms, a person needs to see a brand as many as seven times before booking/ordering.

Measure the effectiveness of various Advertising

It is a good idea to create a monitoring system to evaluate the success of the various types of advertising. You will want to make sure that you have achieved your objectives:

- How many responses did you receive to a particular advert?
- How many of these enquiries became sales?
- What was the value?

One basic way is to create a table via Word or an Excel spreadsheet with all your advertising methods to track these results. You will need to find out in some way from your guests how they heard about you and if any came through any of these advertising methods. If you have no clue as to how effective your advertisements are and you have no way of finding out, then think again about advertising there. Your whole team need to be on board to find out how enquirers and guests found out about you, whether they ask at reception and record (via registration), ask in general conversation or through email tools such as the contact form. You could design your website so that you have specific landing pages when you are running a certain promotion so you can track the Internet traffic.

Part five: Marketing and business success

Accommodation pricing structure

In order to decide what is the most appropriate pricing structure for renting out your holiday accommodation, it is best to do some research first. You need to establish a pricing policy as a priority as it influences your profitability. If your prices are too high, prospective guests will think that you are too expensive, and too low, they will think that there must be something wrong. We monitor our pricing structure every year. We check our prices against our competitors and feel we are priced 'right' for what we offer and our position in the market place. We run many promotional campaigns, offer and discounts throughout the year, so many of our guests receive a discount. If your prices are already very low, then you will receive low yield management (minimised revenue). When the demand for accommodation is low, then occupancy is low and therefore it makes sense to lower your prices. Our low season is April and May; medium season is June and September. Where demand is high for accommodation (July and August) we increase our prices to reflect this.

Target your potential customers!

You can conduct market surveys/questionnaires and target populations which would be interested in staying with you either by direct targeting such as asking people off the street or sending out mail shots, or newsletters or phoning people (if you have postal addresses, phone numbers) or via the Internet (if you have email addresses). Nowadays, social media such as face book, and twitter or other social networking groups such as LinkedIn are widely used by businesses to promote their business. Or you can create a blog via your website and update frequently to show what is happening at your glampsite in terms of promotions/offers or share photos of events and guests enjoying themselves. It is good to use a mix of approaches and methods to cover the widest area possible.

Who are your customers?

Now that you have gathered your market data from various sources (qualitative and quantitative) and analysed the results, you need to make an evaluation of who you believe are your target customers.

Working out the demographic of your customers is highly useful. You can see which are the majority of the people who fall in a certain age group, occupational category, which country, interests/hobbies, and whether they are single, couples or in families, and so much more information.

> We find that we seem to mostly appeal to families with young children before the teenage years, as we have a children´s play area, a pond with fish, and chickens that they can feed. We have a friendly dog and cats and a small, fenced swimming pool, safe for children to swim in if they are accompanied by an adult. Our countryside environment can offer children an adventure which they might not feel at a hotel or in an apartment block.

We have found that our guests tend to come from the UK (50%), Holland (15%), Germany (10%), Portugal (10%), Spain (5%), France (5%) and the rest of world (5%).

We have a mixture of couples in the 20–45 age group and families in the 25–50 age group. We have occasional groups of all ladies, 20–40 age group, or groups of friends, 20–40 age group, and on rare occasions solo travellers, 20–45 age group. We very rarely have over-60-year-olds stay with us; if they do they tend to be in a family group and often stay in the cottage, as it is cool and very comfortable, with private facilities. Also, we state on our website that the glampsite has a lot of uneven ground to walk on so is unsuitable for the elderly or people with walking disabilities.

GLAMPING AS A BUSINESS

It is very difficult to push or operate a wheelchair around our site, so the site is unsuitable for people who are in a wheelchair. The average age range is 20–50 years. Of course we have many babies and children staying with us, from 6 months to 18 years old. The average age range of children staying with us is 3–14 years old.

Research your competition – Find out who your direct competitors are.

> *I view my strongest competition as myself. You're always trying to top yourself, rather than worrying about what other people are doing.*
>
> *John C. Reilly*

It is paramount that you look at what your competition is charging for similar accommodation. If you decide to be higher priced than them then you need to justify why. You may decide you have more facilities on offer, in a better location, for example close to a beach, or your standard overall regarding accommodation is higher. Glamping is still very subjective and can be difficult to categorize in terms of AA stars, but common sense tells you where you fit in terms of campsite standards and star ratings so that is a good gauge.

If you decide to be the cheapest and undercut all your competition then this can scream to potential customers: What is wrong with this glampsite, why are they so cheap? Plus you need to consider the financial implications of being the cheapest. Can you afford to do that? As an example to illustrate this point: We have noticed that when it is winter time, very low season in the Algarve, with very few tourists around, a lot of restaurants will offer very cheap set menus. Suddenly, the menu price gets lower and lower, because there is a pricing war between some of the restaurants competing to go the lowest. Six months later you see some of these restaurants closed. It may not have been viable to buy the ingredients, cook and serve meals on the premises (costs of rent, electricity, gas, taxes etc.) for that price without making any profit.

Top Tip

When you start to undervalue yourself, your product or your service, so will everybody else!

Also, you do not want to undervalue what you are offering. For example, we set the price for a 1-hour massage at €40, which is the average price for a massage in the Algarve; however, many 4- or 5-star spa hotels charge €60–80 per hour. Of course, you are paying for the quality of the environment, as well as the quality and experience of a trained therapist, so it is understandable the price will reflect that. We could charge less, at €30–35, as some local places in the area charge, but we decided that €40 was the right price for us and this is what a massage was worth. We ensure our therapists are qualified and experienced enough to give good treatments. Also, we did not want people having a massage just because it was the cheapest place to get one in the area.

Of course people are looking for good value and are savvy with researching and finding the best deals. So, they will look at your competition and compare your glampsite to others in the area. All of this needs to be taken into account with pricing your accommodation at a fair price for you and your customers.

Offering appropriate activities

Once you have worked out who your guests are and what your guests are most likely to enjoy doing at your glampsite or nearby, you can source appropriate local activities, sports, or excursions. As we are in a very popular tourist area, we have a lot of choice for a variety of activities so we have over the years offered information such as brochures /flyers in our chill-out lounge. Guests have fed back to us what they felt about their experience of a certain activity in terms of enjoyment, price etc., so we have then decided to recommend that activity or excursion, which is detailed in our welcome pack folder of information, and we have a 'things to do' sign and a notice board with posters.

Of course we are very happy to speak to guests directly when they ask us what activities we would recommend.

Working with business partners: Commission arrangements

Once we feel that enough guests have provided positive feedback to us about an activity or an excursion, we would then speak to the business who are running the activity or excursion and let them know we are promoting, advertising and recommending them to our guests and ask them if they would like to form a business partnership with a commission structure.

We have found that there are many businesses in the Algarve who are very slow in seeing the mutual value and benefit of working together in this way, and many places have refused to offer any commission even though we send them many of our customers! Having said that, we have formed some good partnerships where we have a commission agreement in place, such as car hire companies and taxi services, who will give us a percentage of the service sold and they will advertise or promote us on their website or through recommending us via word of mouth.

Update your website regularly!

There are so many new competitors springing up all the time, with new slick-looking websites wishing to look better than you, so it is really important that you stay ahead of the game and keeping information up to date (or it will confuse your website readers) by continuously updating photos, changes in accommodation, new facilities, and new price changes and promotional offers.

It is like redecorating your bedroom after so many years: just by painting a few walls and changing the bed cover and cushions, it makes it look brighter and fresher, and does not cost a huge amount of money or time to do it. You can pay a web designer to do it for you or you can do it yourself (which will save you a lot of money). There are many good DIY website books available to buy, or you could go on a short crash course or hire someone who has some basic web know-how and good administration skills, if you have a fairly simply designed website which is user friendly.

> ## Top Tip
>
> Remember if your website looks out of date then so does your business!

If you have a blog on or attached to your website then it is beneficial to have this updated regularly with photos of guests who have stayed with you or of staff having a great time; even information on forthcoming events or events that have taken place, what is happening around your local area and things to do. In the winter, when we undertake projects, we often put up photos showing the progress of these projects, as we find that previous guests are really interested to see what is evolving on our glampsite or potential guests can see that work is being done to improve facilities etc.

Search engine optimisation

Now, hopefully your website will have had some time to have gained a good position within web pages in various search engine results, e.g. Google and Bing. You are aiming to be on page 1 of a search engine such as Google. Of course this can change day-to-day or week to week if you have been searching your website name to see where it comes up in Google searches. This will depend on so many variables, but obviously you want to be visible to potential customers and high up above your competitors. As part of your Internet marketing strategy, search engine optimisation (SEO) includes what people search for and their actual search terms or key words typed into the search engines and which engines are preferred by your target audience. To get maximum optimisation from your website, continuously edit its content, including any blogs and social media websites such as Facebook. You can perform more detailed analyses as to where, how and why you are positioned in Google searches by using the Google Analytics tool.

121

You need to sign up to Google Analytics by creating a login name (you will need your website address and email) and password, and then you can carry out many different investigations, such as how people found your website e.g. Face book This is very useful to know from an advertising perspective. If you have been spending money and time on certain websites you advertise on and they appear high up in Google Analytics, then you know that it is worth staying with them.

Measuring business success – Bookings and sales

As with all holiday accommodation, there will be low seasons and high seasons, usually revolving around holiday seasons, especially school holidays. We open April to October, and although we find that Easter can be quite busy, traditionally April is quiet, with only a small number of bookings. May is also usually quiet (which is such a shame, because the site looks really beautiful with so many wild flowers and often a lot of sun). However, May bank holidays can be good, depending on flight prices. June starts to pick up, with more national bookings, that is, Portuguese people desiring long weekends, and so early June usually has some bookings, and then from mid-June onwards we often receive a lot of bookings. July and August are traditionally fully booked and September is good, with a lot of bookings.

This pattern therefore reflects that we have a low season, which is April and May; June and September is our medium-season months, and high season is July and August. We often run discounts to reflect these seasonal prices.

It is useful and helpful to use some sort of analytical tool to analyse and evaluate your bookings and sales for the year at the end of season.

There are many off-the-shelf software packages which hotels or businesses within the hospitality industry use. Or you can use software applications for accounts or create your own using Excel spreadsheets for calculating sales, turnover and profit. If you employ an accountant they can also do this for you.

As with setting up and running any business, it is a rule of thumb that it can take at least 5 years for your business to start making any profit. But there are so many other factors and variables involved that it can take longer. Setting up a glamping site requires a lot of financial investment, and so it may be many years before you see any return on your investment.

Top Tip

If you are at the point in your business where you do not need to pay for advertising anymore because you can rely on your word-of-mouth recommendations, then you really are running a successful business in terms of customer satisfaction!

Customer satisfaction

Find out whether your customers enjoyed their stay

There are many ways you can find out whether your guests genuinely enjoyed their stay with you.

One way is by asking them on the day they are leaving or checking out. Some people will always be polite and nice to your face and say... 'Yes, it was great, we really enjoyed our stay.' Then the next thing you realise is that they wrote a negative review about their experience on a reviewing website such as Trip Advisor. This can be really hard to swallow, as you may have tried to do your best to communicate with them by asking them during their stay or emailing afterwards.

We have provided customer feedback forms for our guests in the welcome packs and in our chill-out lounge, so people can complete them anonymously or not. Some people complete on checking out, which is very helpful to us because we can then analyse this information and see what was good, bad and ugly, and how we can improve for the following year.

Top Tip

Some people feel too uncomfortable to tell you the truth in a direct way such as face to face or via email. We are in the hospitality business and so sometimes we just have to accept this fact, just as you cannot please everyone no matter how hard you try!

Some people make what we sometimes regard as ridiculous suggestions (just not do-able), while others point out areas which we also saw needed improving and we felt would be for the benefit of most if not all our customers, but did not have the time or resources to do it that year; or perhaps it was a new problem area that was drawn to our attention.

We also email all guests once they have left, thanking them for staying with us and asking if we could have done anything to have made their stay better.

We also receive feedback from various review websites: Booking.com and Trip Advisor, and people are free to provide feedback on Facebook about their experience staying with us.

When we receive enquiries from people mentioning friends or family who have recommended us to them, then we know we are definitely doing something positive and this word-of-mouth recommendation is by far the most satisfying to receive as anyone who owns a business will tell you! (Plus it is free advertising!)

Increasing revenue

Ways to boost your sales and income

There are many ways you can increase revenue. One way is by increasing your prices, but you will need to review what your competitors are charging and whether you can justify a price increase. Inflation is one reason why businesses have to increase their prices. Another way of increasing revenue is to offer additional services such as food and drink, by way of a bar, cafe or restaurant.

Of course you need to make sure you have the appropriate licences in order to operate and have the staff (a cook or chef, serving staff etc.) so you will be increasing your salary bill.

You will need to assess the likelihood of guests eating in your restaurant – Is it far away from other eating establishments? Are you already offering self-catering accommodation?

We conducted a lot of surveys on guests staying with us and we asked them if we had a cafe how often would they use it. Many said breakfast only, and some said the occasional evening meal; very few said lunch. This is because we offer basic private camp kitchens for our guests, who on the whole want to cook or are happy to have that facility available to them.

We have run yoga retreats ourselves and by other teachers. As a holistic therapist and yoga teacher, I found it generally easier running them myself, because there is a lot of administration involved in organising a retreat: communication, taking the bookings, answering each individual's requests, and providing additional support and facilities for the group. The worst scenario you can find yourself in, is when you organise a retreat being run by a third party and then at the 11th hour they cancel because they haven't enough delegates to attend their course. In essence, any large group booking, be it a wedding or retreat, although it can bring in lucrative revenue, can also bring great big headaches!

Most of our guests have cars and go out during the day to the beach or to explore the Algarve and its many attractions; they have lunch out or they take a packed lunch made in their camp kitchens. We have on average 25–30 guests during high season and so we might be lucky to have 10 or so having breakfast or enjoying an evening meal with us. It is just not viable for us to offer this service for our guests. We also do not wish to open to the public, but, if

126

we did, then it could be viable for us to run a cafe or restaurant.

You could look at increasing revenue via having guests attend events and workshops that you have available at your site. We have run several 1-day workshops, run by myself and others. For example, a 1-day gong meditation workshop was very successfully organised, with an excellent turnout. It took a lot of organisation, but it was worth it. We advertised on Facebook, on our blog a few weeks before the event and emailed guests who would be staying with us at that time, as well as having a black board in our chill-out lounge a few days before the event; and small flyers were put in each accommodation.

You could accept special group bookings such as wedding parties, which can bring in a large sum of revenue but that require a lot of time, effort, organisational skills and resources; and you have to decide whether they have exclusive use of the whole site without any other guests staying or whether they are prepared to share some of the facilities with other guests. You also need to consider the other guests: whether they are comfortable staying while there is a big, potentially noisy event going on around them.

After judging your profit margins and reflecting on what has happened during the course of the year on your site – customer experience and satisfaction, problems and solutions to improve the physical site and business side – then you may feel in a position to plan the forthcoming season.

If you feel the time is right to expand your site with regard to more accommodation units or more facilities, then you need to assess your financial situation. If you want to expand by putting in more accommodation units, you need to work out the costs for installing them, which include buying the units or materials to make/build them, as well as installing them.

You also need to take into consideration whether your site's existing land and facilities can accommodate more units. You also need to talk to the relevant authorities about upgrading the existing infrastructure, electricity supply, water supply, sewerage, access, security, and health and safety. It may be that when you investigate further you find out that the current electrical supply is only sufficient for the existing number of accommodation units. We experienced this with tripped switches, and so cables had to be upgraded.

Another example to illustrate this point is that we initially had one shower /toilet block which had two showers/toilets in the ladies and two for the men. Our staff (manager and volunteers who lived on site) also used it with the guests. When we expanded to include a few more accommodation units, we decided to build an additional bathroom next to our manager's accommodation for the use of the manager and volunteers) to free up the communal block. The upside was that our staff received new facilities to enjoy and so we were also raising the level of satisfaction for our staff as well as our customers.

Chapter 4

Looking After Your Guests

Prior to guests' arrival

Before your guests arrive it is necessary that you have provided all the relevant information for them and of course answered all their questions appropriately.

You will receive enquiries via phone, email and by people arriving unannounced on site, so therefore face to face.

Phone calls

We have our business mobile phone number available on site. This number is usually given to our managers to use as they are on the frontline, meeting and greeting guests on a daily basis and often have to explain how to find us when guests have difficulty finding the glampsite. They are expected to answer calls during their working hours and on their days off we are given the mobile phone to manage. When our glampsite is open, our team can receive calls from people enquiring if there is any accommodation available, and most of the time they can be last-minute bookings because the enquirer is already in Portugal and wanting to book in the next few days; therefore it is important to answer all calls in a polite and helpful manner, write down the enquiry details, and call back if it is inconvenient to talk at that moment. We always ask phone enquirers to email us their enquiry, as it is a lot easier providing them availability and quoting the price, taking the payment, asking them to complete a booking form, emailing directions and recording them on our arrival spread sheet etc.

Top Tip

It's vital that you have some type of checklist in place for your team to ensure that all the relevant and necessary documents have been sent out to the guests before their arrival date and that you have received all the required information from them. Our booking forms act as a tool to check that we have all the information we need. Nothing is more stressful or embarrassing than if guests arrive and you have no information about who they are and when they were expected. It screams poor customer service!

Email

We spend a lot of time dealing with enquiries through to

guest arrival via the company email account. We have an administration process in place with an administration training manual for the office team and operation team to use. There are hotel computerised systems in place which will facilitate generating the appropriate automated email from enquiry through to guest arrival information, which should help minimise your administration. Of course you may never escape direct emails from prospective guests or guests due to arrive, as they may have questions to ask you that your website, FAQs etc. somehow do not answer (or they somehow missed the information). It is important to maintain the right balance of being available to answer questions, so you are giving a personalised customer service, with a more impersonal approach that computerised systems will provide. If you provide an on-line accommodation calendar showing availability and then a booking facility, this can help cut back some administration, because guests can see for themselves when there is availability, and book and pay for the accommodation via the on-line calendar.

Unannounced visitors

There will be times when you have people arrive on site enquiring whether there is accommodation available and whether they could look around the site. As we do not publish our exact address on our website and only give out detailed directions to confirmed guests, we actually receive relatively few enquirers of this nature. Our view is that we want our guests to feel that they are in a special 'hideaway' place, not at a place where the general public can freely wander in and out, which can happen in some establishments. We do not have enough time to give tours around the glampsite. We feel it is important to respect the privacy of our guests and so place a limit on tours for unannounced visitors who might have no intention of booking accommodation with us.

Booking and Cancellation Policy – Booking Policy Terms and conditions

It should be made clear on your website what your terms and conditions are with regard to your booking policy and also on the booking form that guests complete and sign, because it is an agreement (the accommodation you are offering and the price) between you and the guests. Unfortunately every year a few guests cancel their holiday for a variety of reasons, so we have detailed that in the unfortunate event they cancel their holiday we cannot refund the money that they paid for accommodation. One year we received six cancellations. It is up to you what you feel is a fair cancellation policy (you can always look at what other glampsites do on their websites), but this must be clearly communicated through your website, emails, literature and booking forms.

Guests' arrival

Smooth system for check-in

On the day of your guests' arrival, you should have effective and efficient systems in place so that their arrival is a comfortable and smooth one. We have computerised systems producing paper printouts of guests' arrival information, and also a folder in chronological order containing guest booking forms.

Our operations team of management and volunteers who clean and make the glamping accommodation ready for the guests also have a copy of this information in advance so that they can be organised to get the units ready on time for check-ins. Each morning, the operations team and office team look at the arrival schedule and booking forms to ensure we are all ready for the days' arrivals. In an ideal world, you will have all the information you need many days in advance, but even with the best efforts in place some guests are impossible to contact and will not get back to you with all the information that you need. You can only do your best to send out directions, contact numbers etc. and hope that they call you or arrive having used all the information that you provided for them.

Meeting and greeting guests

Once the guests arrive on the site, there is a welcome board with the guests' names and the accommodation they are staying in and our contact numbers. Usually the managers or a member of the team is on hand to welcome the guests. The guests are taken to their unit first so that they can see that all is good and, should there be any issues with their accommodation, camp kitchen etc., these can be raised immediately and dealt with quickly. Then they are shown around the site and taken to the reception area for check-in and guest registration. At this point, fire and general safety are spoken about, as well as the facilities and any events or workshops that may be taking place during their stay.

We also draw their attention to the guests' welcome folder of information which is in all glamping units and details in sections: health and fire safety, map of the site, facilities available on site, things to do on site and off site, local area:

shops, cafes and restaurants and various beaches, markets etc. You may decide that it is a good idea to offer your guests a complimentary welcome drink on arrival at reception or in their accommodation, or at a social event that you offer for all new guests to meet and socialise.

Offering additional services – Providing welcome packs, taxis and sundries

There is an opportunity to offer many types of services to your guests, which can be chargeable or complimentary. You will need to work out which services add value to your guests and which will not, e.g. we considered offering a sauna or hot tub for our guests to use. We looked into the costs of running, cleaning and maintaining them etc. and decided that we would charge guests to use them, but as they are a chargeable facility we felt that we would not have a large uptake. Other services can range from providing welcome packs (we charge for a breakfast pack on arrival) or meals such as breakfast if you market yourself as a B&B or providing lunch or dinner.

We recommend and provide contact details of a transfer company from the airport to our site, where the guests pay the transfer company direct, who also provide a local taxi service. Massage and yoga are available at a charge.

Towels are charged at €5 per towel, but some establishments will provide them as complimentary (but be aware of the ecology of the environment and costs for laundry). Some glampsites charge for additional cleaning to take place while a guest is staying. We do not charge; however, in our welcome pack, we explain that we are eco-conscious and will offer a complimentary clean inside their accommodation unit after five nights if they have booked longer than seven nights.

Housekeeping and cleaning

Our operations team of management and volunteers are responsible for ensuring that all the accommodation units, including their private camp kitchens and dining areas, and all facilities that guests and staff use are cleaned and maintained every day. We have a rota in place that our managers are responsible for producing weekly, ensuring it is adhered to by coaching and supervising the volunteers as well as working alongside them. All volunteers are trained properly by our management as part of their induction process and the management team are there to support the team to ensure all housekeeping and cleaning tasks are carried out on time and of the highest quality. We have a training manual on how to carry out the various housekeeping and cleaning tasks, which all volunteers are expected to read as part of their induction and training.

Top Tip

Remember you cannot please all the people all the time; the best thing you can do is to try and learn from these complaints and intend to show that you are continuously improving by carrying out improvements to the site.

Carrying out site maintenance work

All glampsites inevitably will have routine maintenance work that needs to be carried out, and then there will be unexpected work that will also need to be done. A maintenance manager carries out most of the work around the site. From time to time he may also call in other professionals depending on the problem needing repairing. It is vital that when you receive a complaint, for example 'There is no water in the showers', that your team act quickly to alert the maintenance team so they can fix the problem as soon as possible.

When our site is closed during the winter months, we carry out a lot of maintenance work such as painting buildings, repairing facilities, improving facilities or undertaking new building work. Be prepared to carry out maintenance work throughout the year!

Dealing with customer complaints

It is not pleasant having to deal with complaints from customers, but in any business, especially within hospitality, it is expected. Many guests will seem no trouble at all; all is well and you receive positive feedback throughout their stay and when you follow up in an email afterwards. Other guests will arrive and, from that moment on, it can seem you are spending a lot of your time trying to rectify any issue or problem they have told you about.

Some people may never seem to be satisfied whatever you do for them, but all complaints should be sorted out as quickly as possible, especially if you have good systems in place and a good maintenance person available. It is imperative that you always apologise for any problems that your guests have encountered (even if it does not seem justified) and let them know you are acting as quickly as possible to rectify the problem. Always, check with them later that the problem is fixed and they are now happy!

It great to celebrate positive feedback with your team as it helps raise morale and can act as a thank you for all their efforts and hard work. Of course not everyone is going to tell you the truth to your face, as they may feel more comfortable doing this via email, which is why it is important to follow up via email afterwards with all guests. You could include this positivity on your website, blog and social media as testimonials. If you have a Visitors Book, and you have people writing positive messages, you could display them also. People will also write reviews on the Internet, both positive and negative, and on travel sites such as Trip Advisor.

At the end of the season we analyse and evaluate all feedback and consolidate it and discuss as a team how we can learn from this and make improvements for the next year. It is easy to dwell on the two or three individuals who seemed to endlessly complain during their stay and may have even left early when actually 200 people were generally happy or very happy staying with you during the season, so the actual percentage of people hating their stay was very small. All hotels and campsites receive complaints, even those with top ratings. So remember to celebrate your successes!

Damage Policy

It is inevitable that your site will receive damage from guests, most likely caused by accidents. You could take a 'damage' deposit off them before or when they arrive and then on check-out (after a quick inspection of their accommodation unit) return their deposit. You will need to make sure you have cash on site if you return their deposit on the day of departure or you may choose to return their deposit on-line via bank transfer or PayPal.

Guests' demographic profile

As you will experience, in a people-type business such as this type, there are many different types of guests from different countries, cultures, ages, backgrounds etc., which can make life really interesting when you meet and talk with them. After your first season you can look back on which months had the most solo travellers, groups, couples, friends and families. This is useful information in planning for the next season in terms of discounts for certain accommodation and knowing which accommodation most appeals to a special group.

For example, May is traditionally a quiet month for us and usually with a lot of couples and young families with babies or very young children under 5 years old. Often we offer couples a free upgrade or another discount to stay in the larger family units which are often available then.

Animal Policy – On site and other peoples pets

This covers the animals you have on site (farm animals or kept enclosed as in a zoo) and your pets, as well as whether to allow other animals or pets on site to visit or stay. We currently have one dog and four cats that we see as part of our family and therefore our pets. We also have chickens, with a hutch, and koi carp fish in a large pond, in a large, caged enclosure. Our neighbour lends us his goats during the summer season so that the children can enjoy feeding them. We do not allow other people's pets on site because it can upset the balance in our own pets and we want our pets to feel happy in their own home.

Departures

Guests' check-out

On the day of your guests' check-out, a process or system should be in place so thatthey leave their holiday with you on a positive note. Our managers check out all guests and are happy to extend their check-out time if we do not have guests arriving until later that day or the following day. We will happily allow people to put their luggage in the chill-out lounge or even let them put their food in the guests' fridge in the chill-out lounge and let them use the facilities until they leave. It is a good idea to ask them beforehand when they are departing, date and time, so you can build this into your administrative schedules for planning the next arrivals, especially if they are on the same day. We ask them at the booking stage, when they complete the booking form, and again via email if they have not told us, the time they are leaving on the departure date.

Guests' aftercare

When guests leave its important to ensure you do all you can to stay in touch positively and encourage them to come back and stay again and tell their friends and family to stay with you. As I mentioned earlier, we send out a thank you email offering discounts for them if they decide to return and also for anyone who books that they recommend us to. Also, if they offer constructive feedback about making improvements to the site or customer service then, this should be responded to positively. If they do return it is always good to follow up on all previous emails, correspondence and booking forms etc., so that when they arrive again your team are prepared to meet them with a very special VIP welcome.

Chapter 5

Looking after yourself

> ### Top Tip
>
> The key is to try and strike the right balance for you so you feel happy with the work, rest and play ratio.

Your Health

No matter how demanding your business is, your health should never suffer because of it. It can be difficult to quantify how a business can cause ill health problems as it can often be a number of years before symptoms show up either mentally, emotionally or in a physical way. Stress really does play a big part in many of today's illnesses and diseases. If your business is causing you a huge amount of stress, then this could eventually cause some form of disease within you. As an example, if you are a workaholic and work all hours driving your business forward, your personal life could suffer as a result. Your loved ones may feel very upset and distressed with you and this may lead to breakdowns in relationships which ultimately will cause you to suffer emotionally and physically.

Poor diet, lack of sleep, lack of exercise or too much

exercise can all lead to health problems so balance is key to all these areas. Eat healthily: on a daily basis, plenty of vegetables fruits, proteins and complex carbohydrates, which will provide a balanced and nutritious diet, and will give you more energy and help boost your immune system, staving off colds and other infections. Quite often you can have so many thoughts running around your head, especially relating to your business, that it can feel impossible to switch off from them and get to sleep early.

Having warm baths, drinking warm milk or calming herbal teas such as chamomile and not drinking caffeine after midday can all help promote a good night's sleep.

Turn off your computer at least 2 hours before bed, and reading a book can also help. Likewise if you have too much sleep then you can feel lethargic and not feel motivated to do much, which can be a sign of depression. If we are desk bound for a lot of the day and not freely moving around, then we suffer from lack of exercise, sunlight and clean oxygen that the outside air will provide, so it is good to take small breaks throughout the day if you are working in an office and get outside and go for a walk.

Ignoring health issues will only lead to potentially worse problems, so if you feel that something is not right with your health and you feel out of balance then addressing these concerns as soon as possible is important. Visit your doctor and, if it feels appropriate, a complimentary practitioner can also help. For example, during winter months, people can suffer from Seasonal Affective Disorder (SAD) due to lack of natural light.

Ill health can eventually lead to further debilitation where you may not be well enough to work, and ultimately your business will also suffer, as well as those close to you of course.

Your personal and social life

Looking after you

Like anyone running their own business, it can feel like it consumes your whole life, especially in the early years, when it seems that every waking minute of the day is spent thinking about your business! This is normal and can even be positive as it drives you forward to accomplish new business goals and successes. However, it should not come at the cost of your health or your family.

Some days it may feel like it is just work, work, work, with little time to do anything else, especially during the peak tourist season. The goal is to get to a point where systems are streamlined and working well, and you are able to delegate a lot more to your team so you have more free time to do something you enjoy that is unrelated to work; or maybe you just want to take some time out away from your business to relax. By being able to do this, you will find that you will feel happier and more relaxed even in the busier, tourist season. It can cause some people to experience guilty feelings walking away offsite, leaving the team to work while you relax, but in the long term everyone will benefit so there is no need to feel guilty.

If you feel that you are fair as an owner/leader and allow your team enough time off, then why shouldn't you feel entitled to it as well? There may seem to be an expectation from the world of business that if you are the owner (especially with an entrepreneurial spirit) that you should be seen to spend every waking hour at your business to show dedication to your team.

If you are very tired, stressed and feeling frazzled by work demands, then this can be projected onto your team and be counterproductive. Despite workloads, and even work crises that unexpectedly seem to arrive and overwhelm you, try to stop, take a breath, focus and then re-prioritise what is essential right now, and put the rest on hold or delegate some work to other team members. You could leave the site for a short time to take a break and clear your mind, so when you return you are feeling refreshed and refocused, ready to tackle any challenges.

It is so easy to get consumed by business demands that, even when you are invited by friends or family to do something, you decline because of the demands of the business. Of course during the peak summer season it is understandable that you will have less time available for socialising, but it is still possible to have a positive social life, it just requires good organisation and delegation with your team.

It is not surprising that in the Algarve during the summer months many people who work in tourist businesses find themselves very busy with work, often working long unsociable hours, and declining so many interesting events (even if financially they are able to take part); then in the winter when it is a very low tourist season and many businesses close, people have a lot more time to enjoy themselves and go out; there are fewer events, but many people choose not to go out much for fear of spending their savings they worked so hard for during the summer season to help them through the winter.

Top Tip

As well as looking after the Business you also need to think about looking after you. Easier said than done!

We encourage our managers and team of volunteers to be friendly and sociable towards our guests, because they tend to hang out in the chill-out lounge, where guests and our team can enjoy socialising together. Once a week there is a communal BBQ to encourage a social atmosphere for both guests and our team. We also respect that some people are less sociable and may not enjoy socialising in the communal areas as much as other guests, and this can apply to staff as well so it is important to recognise this and respect people's privacy.

However, you do not always need a lot of money to go out to enjoy yourself. We are lucky that we live near beautiful countryside and quaint villages and towns and only 10 minutes from great beaches. So if we are feeling energetic, we can go for great walks or hikes around lakes, hills and beaches or just enjoy the drive in the car. There are markets and fairs, and often exhibitions of art, which are all free. As we have more time in the winter, we can catch up with friends and invite them around for dinner or vice versa, or go out for a local cheap meal.

Doing things you enjoy such as hobbies, interests, sports, courses or leisure pursuits will have the added benefit of personal development. Learning new skills will make you feel more confident, but this can also be a bonus in that it could be helpful for your business as it may be a skill that can be transferred over to benefit your business as well. You may decide in the future that you can spend more time doing these hobbies alongside running your business, or it could be that you can make money from doing other pursuits/running another business alongside your business or do other paid/unpaid work. This can all be possible if you can delegate well and have a really good, supportive team that you can trust while you are pursuing other areas of interest.

Top Tip

So no matter how sociable and friendly you feel towards guests, viewing socialising as an important part of customer care, know where to draw the line between what is appropriate behaviour with guests and being professional.

The other added benefit of enjoying socialising is that it can further develop your interpersonal skills, and networking opportunities can present themselves to you as you are meeting more people. These could be work related and so you might benefit by meeting new contacts that could help your business or just meet new people to hang out and have fun with, which will enrich your personal life and you will feel like a happier person.

Should you hang out with your guests? For some, for example, it is great fun going to a local restaurant that you recommend so you can all enjoy the typical local cuisine or hang out in bars and let your hair down dancing the night away together. However, there is a professional line that needs to be considered.

Do you want to wake up the next morning with an enormous hangover and clueless to what happened the previous night with your guests in case you got up to something embarrassing! It is not like at the work Christmas Party where people often laugh about the previous night's events with light-hearted humour and then it is forgotten. If a guest disapproves or feels offended in some way, they may decide to write a review about their experience on a review website such as Trip Advisor. You may decide to have some rules or a Code of Conduct policy for your team where you discourage any personal, intimate relations between guests and your staff and or between staff; whatever feels appropriate and comfortable for your business.

Striking a good balance with living on site

When you live on site, whether your home is right in the heart of the glampsite and you are visible to guests or whether it is more hidden away, expect to be accessible to your guests and team workers, who might knock on your door and ask for assistance. You may feel you never get a moment's peace, even during your 'designated' time off. This can make it difficult to relax in your own home so you may feel you cannot walk around for long in your bath robe in case somebody knocks on your door. If you live off site, then the geographical separation of your home and business at least can help you to switch off psychologically from the business, but it would be convenient to live within 10 minutes' drive from the site. As an example, if you live above your business, as in the case of a flat above a shop, it may be easier to switch off because you are only available during the opening hours of your shop. Once you have guests on site, it is potentially a 24-hour operation.

Top Tip

Consider making your home as private and as separate from the business as much as possible by putting up a fence around it with gates and an intercom or live offsite very nearby.

Switching off and well-being strategies - Finding ways to switch off from the business

Finding ways to switch off from the business is crucial to your overall wellbeing, which will affect those around you. These will vary from person to person, but here is a list that may help:

- Set a time each day when you will not be at your desk or on the computer and stick to it.

- Set a time each day when you will not discuss business matters with your partner or family.

- Turn off your mobile phone or put the landline number on answering machine when you are not working and with your family, especially during meal times.

- Set a time for a lunch break even a short 30 minutes so you can really enjoy something delicious and healthy to eat.

- Ensure you set small breaks away from your desk (if you are office bound a lot) to get out and walk around outside to get fresh air and get your body moving. It may be a good idea to set some breaks around needing to go to another part of the site to speak to a member of staff or guest so it forces you out away from your desk.

- Equally if you are very 'operational' and hands on and always in a workshop or doing back-breaking work in a garden around the site, ensure you have enough small breaks to sit down and relax for a few minutes and refuel if necessary.

- Communicate clearly to your team when you are not available, such as weekends or a certain day as you are with your family or have your day off (only contactable in an emergency); you may also want to tell your guests.

- Take time out away from the business altogether even if only for a few hours, such as going for a walk along the beach or relaxing outside a cafe, going for a nice walk in the countryside by a river or reading a book in a quiet place.

- Try relaxation therapies such as yoga, meditation, Tai Chi, having a massage or receiving other complimentary therapies.

- Enjoy any physical exercise that gets your body moving such as swimming, running, jogging, playing tennis, squash, badminton, aerobics, going to the gym for a workout or a dancing class.

- Join a group who meet up to do a team activity together such as hiking, rowing or playing football.

- Join a class for a workshop or activity such as an art class or renovating furniture, playing a musical instrument, singing or writing.

- Enjoy a relaxing bath with candles or sit in a hot tub.

- Take time away from the business altogether and meet friends or family.

- Go on a holiday even if only a short break for a couple of nights so you can return relaxed, refreshed and recharged.

Taking holidays

Planning holidays away from your business

It can seem impossible to take a holiday especially in the early days of your business due to time constraints and lack of funding (you feel the money is best used in the business first); and you may feel guilty for relaxing on holiday when there is so much work to do.

Planning holidays in advance is crucial so that you can inform your team so they can provide cover. You may decide that you block out a few weeks during the year on your calendar where you do not take guests so that you have a breather even if you do not go away. We have taken the odd weekend break during low season in April when we only have a few guests on site and our team are happy to cover for a few nights. Our neighbours are also vigilant and keep an eye on our place for us when we are away, which is comforting.

Also you may have to plan to find house sitters or arrange for your animals to go into kennels etc. However, my advice is, whether you have farm animals, pets or not, when you own a glampsite, which is usually a large piece of land with property and facilities, there will be security issues to consider. It is necessary to install strong and effective security measures such as an alarm system, high fences and gates with locks and CCTV cameras or employ a security guard.

But having a holiday so that you are away from the business altogether can help you switch off, if only temporarily, so you can really enjoy your holiday. I do not feel I am on holiday unless I am in a different country with little or no reminders of the business. For me, taking a rest at home, sitting in the back garden reading a book when I can look around and see what work needs to be done on the site does not make me feel like I am having much of a holiday and relaxing. Sometimes, when we choose to holiday in places similar to ours (because we like that type of holiday ourselves and also it can help generate new ideas for the business), I can feel we are on a 'busman's' holiday and not fully switch off. That is just the nature of being in the business of holidays and hospitality!

> We go away for our annual long holiday during the winter months when we are closed and we always feel the most relaxed then because we do not have to worry if our Managers are coping well whilst we are not there.

It is funny hearing comments from guests who are staying with us on holiday: 'It must seem like you are always on holiday because you live in a lovely, warm, peaceful place in the countryside with all these facilities'. Yes, it is true, we feel blessed to live in a beautiful part of the world, but we still have to work hard and it is different when you walk around the site seeing all things that are wrong and need work doing to them, than appreciating all the good stuff and beauty around you. I notice these natural beautiful details more, such as a butterfly or apples on a tree, when I am walking around the site in the winter when it is closed. You feel very different then because you can feel more relaxed and can just look at the raw beauty of the landscape, hear and see the birds chirping, the little river whooshing by and wild flowers growing, in harmony without focusing on all the needs of the business.

Arranging House sitters to look after your property, animals and site

As I mentioned earlier, we often ask house sitters to come and stay and look after our animals and our property while we are away. At this point, as the glampsite is closed and all of the tipis, tents and the yurt are all put away, including all furniture and furnishings, all that is left standing are the facilities of the glampsite and our cottage that we rent out to guests. You can find house sitters by paying to join websites that have house sitters registered with them such as www.trustedhousesitters.com or place advertisements on volunteer websites such as WWOOF, Workaway and Help Exchange, or on websites relating to campsite recruitment, vacancy pages or local newspapers When we recruit house sitters we always have a Skype chat first and then ask for references, which we follow up. Then we meet the successful candidate a few days before we leave and show them around the site. I provide them with house-sitting notes and the welcome folder of information that we give to our guests. Our house sitters stay in the cottage and we provide them with basic food provisions and two bikes to use.

Policy for friends and family

Options for personal guests to stay for free

When you own a holiday place in a nice tourist destination, people will often want to come and visit and enjoy having a holiday while coming to see you.

> ## Top Tip
>
> If you have neighbours who can check on your place and provide a 'presence' then that is very helpful, or guard dogs that can be fed by your neighbours or friends also provide effective security.

You may wonder which of your friends and family are coming to see you for a very cheap holiday. However, it is good to consider a family and friends policy where you might give them a very large discount or provide certain accommodation for free at certain times of the year only, when it is low season.

As an alternative you could ask them to contribute in some way, perhaps by physically helping out around the site, or they may prefer to take you out for a nice meal, bring your family presents or leave some money at the end of the stay as a thank you; whatever feels right, but it is important to make the options clear in some way so they do not feel embarrassed by misunderstandings, for example if they thought that they could bring their five-a-side football team to stay for free as well! In this case you might feel it is fair that your family or friend stays for free but their friends get a large discount.

Vision for the future – Looking ahead positively and in balance

In order to feel fulfilled, usually you have to feel happy with your personal and family life, work and health. Most people's visions of the future would be a mixture of all three in order to obtain this happiness. Of course life is full of ups and downs, and we all have to face what life throws at us. Sometimes all three areas are not in balance, but if you were to visualise the future in 5 years' time, all areas of your life would be in a positive balance. You could consider this in a broader sense using a SWOT analysis – Strengths, Weaknesses, Opportunities and Threats – which can help you see what you are good at and enjoy at work and at play, what areas you need to improve or do not like doing and what could be done to create opportunities that could help your business or other areas of your life, as well as outside influences that could cause problems in the business.

You could create a Treasure Map using a mixture of photos, pictures, drawings and words to illustrate your vision of the business and your life for the future over whatever year span feels appropriate to envision. We created a treasure map and framed it and hung it on our wall to look at.

It contained photos of holiday places we would like to visit, photos of relaxation, meditation and massage and words associated such as Zen, wellbeing, happiness and also words such as success, wealth, and photos of projects we would like to build for our glampsite business. You can play around with words, pictures and photos to find what suits you and your vision. It is amazing how you can look back at this map and see all the things you managed to achieve which at the time just seemed like wishful thinking. Your mind is very powerful!

Summary

If you have managed to get this far in your reading, hopefully you are fully aware of the challenges you are likely to face in owning and running your glampsite business.

But as well as gaining knowledge of the practicalities, legalities and finances needed to set up a successful business, one of the most important questions you need to ask yourself is why you want to do it. Is it to earn some income by way of a new business or because you like the idea of the lifestyle –being outdoors and close to nature and enjoy meeting people? However, being an enthusiastic camper and dreaming of the lifestyle it could bring you is just not enough to succeed in a competitive business as this is now. But if you have clear objectives of why you want to do this, what your expectations are, with a clear business strategy supported by effective business and marketing plans and activities, then you should be in a good position to generate successful bookings and sales.

Flexibility is key when responding to external factors in the market place that you have no control over and you it will put you in a good position to make sound business judgements. If you are willing to assess what went wrong, what went well and what you would do differently next year, then you can learn from your mistakes to make improvements for the future. The same applies for looking at ways to increase revenue. Even if you followed all of the advice contained in this book, it does not guarantee you success with your glampsite business. Each business is unique, bringing its own challenges, but if you have a willingness to learn from your mistakes, improve for the future with a lot of positive energy, drive and persistence then this should help you succeed. Establishing a supportive team with good delegating will help you get to a place where you will be able to enjoy your business and downtime.

You are in a people business; it is primarily hospitality, and you rely on a team to help you deliver good customer service. If you are not a people person, then this business may not be for you; however, it is possible to employ management to be the front-of-house operation, to meet guests, then the business will operate successfully. Ultimately, you need to be sure you are happy to share your home with people. If you are not happy doing this then you can create ways to gain more privacy for yourself such as living off site.

Obviously, living off site will guarantee privacy away from the work place. If the enthusiasm starts to wane, then it may be time to move away from the business more and delegate to good managers, or lease it as a franchise or restructure it so that you can feel comfortable and happy working in your business. As with any business, the key to overall success is a good work–life balance: happy working in your business ensuring your guests are happy so they want to return or tell their friends to come, while of course enjoying your private life. Happy glamping!

Appendix 1 – Portuguese Employment Contract Law

Permanent contracts

These give the employee a lot of rights should the employer wish to transfer the employee to another work place; the location should be at the convenience of the employee. There is a 90-day probationary period for most staff and 180 days for staff at management level. Workers who have been with a company for more than 2 years need to give a minimum of 2 months' notice; and, less than 2 years' service, 1 months' notice to resign from their employment. There must be a legitimate objective reason to dismiss an employee.

Fixed term contracts

When compiling a fixed-term contract, it is necessary to have a specific reason for work and duration to justify a short-term contract, e.g. seasonal work such as restaurant or bar work.

Part-time contracts

Part-time workers accrue the same rights and protection as full-time workers. The employment contract should state in writing the daily and **weekly working hours.**

Temporary employees

These workers are employed through a recruitment agency and therefore the agency is responsible for drawing up an employment contract with terms and conditions and paying them direct themselves. They will be available to carry out temporary work for various companies should the agency phone and offer them the work. The agency worker should be available at short notice when the agency calls, but they can agree or turn down the assignment. The advantage for a company to employ a temporary worker through an agency is that, if you feel the worker is not carrying out the work efficiently, then you contact the agency and explain this to them and ask to terminate their contract that same day and ask the agency to find another agency worker as soon as possible. The downside is that the agency worker can also decide they do not want to work for you any more and leave one day without giving you any notice.

Further Information

Arden, P (2003) *It's Not How Good You Are, It's How Good You Want To Be* (Phaidon Press)

Block, P (1990) *The Empowered Manager: Positive Political Skills at Work* (Jossey-Bass)

Coulthard, S (2009) *Shed Chic: Outdoor Buildings for Work, Rest and Play* (Jacqui Small LLP)

Clarke, G and Field-Lewis, J (2013) *Amazing Spaces* (Quadrille)

Cranwell-Ward, J, Bacon, A and Mackie, R (2002) *Inspiring Leadership*

Field-Lewis, J (2012) *My Cool Shed: An Inspirational Guide to Stylish Hideaways* (Pavilion Books)

Goldman, Heinz M (1993) *How To Win Customers* (Pan Books)

Hampshire, D (1998) *Buying a Home in Portugal: A Survival Handbook* (Survival Books)

Harris, C and Borer, P (1998) *The Whole House Book* (Centre for Alternative Technology)

Hill, N, Brierley, J and MacDougall, R (2003) *How To Measure Customer Satisfaction* (Gower)

GLAMPING AS A BUSINESS

Hobbs, G (2008) *Live and work in Portugal* (Vacation Work)

Jones, B (2009) *Building with Straw Bales: A Practical Guide for the UK and Ireland* (Green Books)

Kahn, L (2014) *Tiny Homes on the Move: Wheels and Water* (Shelter)

Kahn, L (2004) *Home Work: Handbuilt Shelter* (Shelter)

Knight, J (2006) *Cool Camping England Guide* (Punk)

Knight, J (2011) *Cool Camping: Glamping Getaways* (Punk)

Lewis, R and Chambers, R (1989) *Marketing Leadership in Hospitality* (Van Nostrand Reinhold)

Lee, V (2013) *Homes from Home: Inventive Small Spaces, from Chic Shacks to Cabins and Caravans* (Jacqui Small LLP)

Liddle, C and Hopping, L (2013) *Handmade Glamping* (CICO books)

Neale, S (2013) *The best Campsites by Waterside in Britain and Ireland* (Adlar Holes)

Olsen, R (2012) *Handmade Houses: A Free-Spirited Century of Earth-Friendly Home Design* (Rizzoli International Publications)

Pearson, D (2000) *The Natural house Book* (Gaia books)

Poincelot, R (1986) *Organic No-Dig, No-Weed Gardening* (Thorsons/Rodale)

Rosen, N (2007) *How To Live Off-Grid* (Bantam Books)

Schwartz, E (2004) *Breakthrough Advertising* (Boardroom)

Weisman, A and Bryce K (2008) Using Natural Finishes : A Step-by-Step Guide (Green Books)

Wilhide, E (2002) *ECO – An Essential Sourcebook for Environmentally Friendly Design and Decoration* (Quadrille)

Wills, D (2012) *Tiny Campsites: Cool Camping* (Punk)

Wheeler, A (2003) *Designing Brand Identity* (John Wiley and Sons)

Courses

There are many courses within the UK (and in other countries) which are relevant to and necessary for this type of business: Health and Safety, Food Handling and Hygiene, First Aid, Customer Care, Hospitality Management, Travel and Tourism, Waiter and Waitress, Barista, Housekeeping and Butler Service.

Useful Websites

Advertisers of glamping sites:

www.alanrogers.com

www.camping.info

www.come-2-portugal.com

www.coolcamping.co.uk

www.glamping-uk.co.uk

www.hideawayportugal.com

www.glampinghub.com

www.goglamping.net

www.glampingeurope.com

www.glamping-holidays.com

www.goglampinginportugal.com

www.glamping.com

www.glampinggetaway.com

www.getonmyland.com

www.quirkyaccom.com

www.oneoffplaces.co.uk

www.peaceful-portugal.com

www.pureportugal.com

www.responsibletravel.com

www.selfcateringbreaks.co.uk

www.uniquesleeps.co.uk

www.ukcampsite.co.uk

General advertisers of accommodation

www.hostelworld.com

www.hostelboookers.com

www.theretreatcompany.com

www.trivago.com

Health and well-being advertisers

www.barefootbuhha.com

www.holistichealth.com

www.on-lineholistichealth.com

www.theonboardspa.com

www.wellbeingjournal.com

www.yogatraveljobs.com

www.yogajournal.com

www.yogatoday.com

Organic gardening/Permaculture

www.globalonenessproject.com

www.organicgardening.com

www.motherearthnews.com

www.planetnatural.com

www.openpermaculture.com

www.permacultureprinciples.com

www.permaculture.org

www.permaculture.net

Volunteer Work exchange websites

www.escapenormaljobs.com

www.interexchange.org

www.WWoofinternational.com

www.workaway.info

www.helpx.net

www.womentravel.info

Business/Marketing related websites

www.anybrowser.com

www.adviceguide.org.uk

www.bestpracticeforum.com

www.businessknowhow.com

www.cipd.co.uk

www.cim.co.uk

www.direct.gov.uk/employment

www.emailaces.com

www.entrepreneur.com

www.franchising.pt

www.british-franchise.org.uk

www.hotelmarketing.com

www.hotelsalessuccess.co.uk

www.hotelcoach.co.uk

www.theidm.com

www.microsoftbusinesshub.com

www.socialmediatoday.com

www.tourismforall.org.uk

www.websitebuilderexpert.com

www.weebly.com

www.wordtracker.com

51420424R00101

Made in the USA
San Bernardino, CA
21 July 2017